nosh
for GRADUATES

Joy May

D1341141

NOSH
BOOKS.COM

Contents

Introduction

As my sons and their friends graduated from student life and student house-sharing, I observed that they wanted a bit more from their food. This gave me the idea to write this book. In the book, I want to help and inspire people, to attempt something a little more adventurous, while, at the same time, keeping things simple.

I have maintained the easy measures of mugs (½ pint) and spoons used in Nosh 4 Students. The star rating indicates the difficulty of the dish. The prices are at the time of writing and give an average price between Sainsburys and Tesco.

We are excited about the Cook School section, which we hope will take a lot of the myth out of cooking and help you to produce some great food.

Moving On

So...you have finished your student days! You had a great time, but want to do things a little differently now. You want to move on from tea and toast round your mate's house and broaden your cooking knowledge and repertoire to something more special. Now you've graduated, you might have a little more money, but not necessarily more time.

The recipes in the book are, on the whole, still quite simple, but with a mix of unique recipes with some different flavours and maybe some ingredients you have not used before. I have tried to use fresh ingredients and as little processed food as possible.

All the recipes have been cooked, recooked and rigorously tested. The taste testers, (our friends and family) fearlessly scored each and every dish, resulting in lots of changes and some dishes not making the final cut.

I have been overwhelmed by the positive response received for our previous books 'Nosh4students' and 'Vegetarian Nosh4students' and I hope you enjoy and, more importantly, use this book just as much.

Store Cupboard

A well stocked store cupboard makes cooking much easier. Don't try to buy everything all at once, as you may buy things you will never use. Rather, buy things gradually as you need to use them and you will soon have a good store. Keep it stocked and you will be able to make impromtu meals when friends call in unexpectedly.

Rosie's Herb Garden

We've all done it, bought a herb pot at the supermarket with good intentions, only to find that when we go to actually use it, that it's withered, gone mouldy and died. The aim of this section is to help you to **grow successful and productive herbs** that can be used in all your favourite recipes.

One of the most important things to know out about your herbs is where they grow naturally. If they originate from Mediterranean soils, it's not surprising that they shrivel and die if over-watered and left on a drafty window sill! **The trick is giving the plants what they want,** or as close as you can get it.

Pots

Before we get onto the herbs themselves, let's start with the basics, beginning with pots. Herbs come from all over the world, so to make sure that they're all happy it's easiest to grow them in individual pots. The benefit of growing them in individual pots is that you can give them the soil and water and environment they prefer. You can remove plants if they are diseased or have a pest problem and you can easily remove annual herbs (ones that last one year) when they are spent and replace with new ones, without disturbing the perennials (the ones that can last for years).

When buying herbs from the supermarket, they often come crammed with seedlings and are overcrowded in their original pots (see picture No.1). This can cause them to go mouldy, or become too pot bound to grow well. Put them into new pots and split the original pot making two plants (see picture No.2 & 3). This will allow them to grow much better and produce more herbs.

When buying thyme from the supermarket, you get a huge amount of tangled leaves and stems. The first thing to do, which seems a little strange, but helps the plant long term, is to cut the plant back drastically and remove the majority of the bushy part (see picture No.4). If possible, use this thyme immediately in a recipe, why not try the Zesty Tuna Steaks on page 89. Before splitting the plant, make sure the soil is moist. This way, it will split more easily and not break so many roots in the process. Having done that, you can more easily split the plant into two pots. Remove the bottom section of the roots, as this will encourage the plant to create new roots and will be healthier for it in the long run (see picture No.5).

Herbs need to be planted in pots with holes in the bottom to allow excess water to drain out. Because of this, you will probably want to sit the pots either on a saucer or a tray. With the exception of the pot you use for chives, it is best to put a handful of gravel or small stones at the bottom of the pots to help with drainage (see picture No.6).

Herb pots should be placed on a bright window sill, preferably out of a draft.

Watering

The thing that kills most herbs is how much we water them. Too little and they dry up and die, too much and they drown. The best way of knowing if you need to water your plant and by how much is to stick your finger into the soil. If your soil feels damp when you touch it and looks dark brown, then you don't need to worry about watering. If the soil is dark, but no longer feels damp, you need to give your plant a little drink.

What about pests?

If you notice any greenfly taking an interest in your plant, the best thing to do is to wash them off under the tap (being careful not to wash away all the compost). These aren't harmful to people, but may not impress your friends when found in the salad!

Pinching out

This is a trick for harvesting and encouraging your plants to be bushier and therefore more productive. When picking from the plant, instead of plucking leaves from the side of the stalk, take the top section of the plant, stalk and all. Nip off just above the next leaf down. This will encourage the plant to re-shoot from this point, usually with more than one shoot (see picture No.7 & 8).

Thyme

WATERING/FEEDING: Avoid watering thyme during the winter, unless it starts to go pale and the leaves drop.

HARVESTING: "Pinch out". Harvest sparingly during the winter.

TRIMMING: To keep your thyme plant in good condition, it is a good idea to give it a light trim after flowering. When trimming thyme, try not to go into the old brown wood, as no new leaves will grow from there. Always try to leave some new green growth with leaves on the plant.

FLOWERING: Allow to flower. This will not affect leaf production.

Rosemary

WATERING/FEEDING: Less picky about when it is watered and doesn't need to always have moist soil. Don't water as much as basil.

HARVESTING: "Pinch out". Harvest sparingly during the winter.

LIFESPAN: Potentially years if looked after.

FLOWERING: Rosemary flowers in late spring, but, because it is a perennial, it doesn't die after flowering. You can leave it to produce very pretty little blue flowers and then carry on harvesting it as before.

Coriander

WATERING/FEEDING: Water only in the mornings.

HARVESTING: "Pinch out" to keep a bushy plant.

LIFESPAN: Less than a year.

FLOWERING: You can collect the seeds from the flowers and plant them, or even use them in recipes. If you don't want to do that, just pinch them out when they form.

Basil

WATERING/FEEDING: Water only in the mornings.

HARVESTING: Use "pinching out" (see previous page).

LIFESPAN: A few months.

FLOWERING: Avoid, as it means your basil is about to die. If this occurs then harvest and use as much basil as possible before it dies. To avoid this, keep your next basil plant as happy as possible!

Things to make life easier when cooking

Build up a store of good cooking equipment and don't be tempted to buy gadgets which usually have limited applications. Request some of them as birthday or Christmas pressies.

Things you should already have:

mug (½ pint)
tablespoon
dessertspoon
teaspoon
sharp knife

peeler
chopping board
non-stick frying pan
wok
large saucepan

medium saucepan
colander
fish slice
grater
baking trays

Additional things that are really good

A good sharp knife makes an amazing difference to your cooking experience. It takes the effort out of chopping and makes it quicker and more effective. Go to a good department store and buy the best knife you can afford. At the same time, buy the appropriate knife sharpener, for the make of knife you decide on. Sharpen the knife every time you use it, it just takes seconds.

One large **'hob to oven' casserole dish** will be very useful; saves decanting from the pan on the hob to a casserole dish. Should have a lid. Especially useful for 'one-pot' dishes.

Good sized casserole dish.

A **big pan** for cooking in quantity.

Silicon spatulas - better and more hygienic than wooden spoons and you can scrape stuff out of the corners of pans and bowls.

Pair of **long handled tongs** are great for turning meat and generally picking food up.

Second chopping board for when friends come to help!

Balloon whisk

Bowls for mixing. Stainless steel ones are easiest to get clean. If you whisk egg whites, for instance, there will be no greasy residue.

Non stick, loose-bottomed cake tin.

Silicon, non-stick sheets - these things are amazing. Costing less than £5 from supermarkets, you can use them over and over as you just wash them in soapy water between uses. Perfect for roasts, biscuits, Pavlovas etc. Things just don't stick to them! No need to grease a baking tray ever again!

A hand-held blender - spend a little more and get one with its own jug, very useful for sauces, smoothies, soups and many other things.

A small **hand-held food mixer** will be very helpful if you want to make Pavlovas and cakes.

COOK SCHOOL

Here we try to take some of the myth out of cooking. Chefs use words, that to a total novice, mean nothing, so we offer some explanation. We also cover some basic cooking skills and offer advice on some problems you may encounter.

What is meant by high, medium and low heats?

All cooking hobs vary. You might have a nice new cooker with a large wok burner hob, or you might have an old cooker, which is less than great, that struggles to heat anything at all! I may tell you to cook on a high, medium or low heat, so how do you know how that translates in your kitchen and your hob?

Here are some guidelines.
When frying, heat the pan first and then add the oil. If the oil 'smokes', then the pan is too hot, if it produces a 'heat haze', it is probably what I would describe as 'hot'. If when you put the food in the oil, it spits at you, it's too hot, if it crackles gently then it's a good high heat. On a medium heat the food should be talking to you a little, bubbling away, but not too fast. On a low heat, things will bubble away very gently.

You may live in rented accommodation and inherit an old cooker. If everything you cook is over or undercooked it may be an idea to buy an oven thermometer (they sell for as little as £4.00) and then work out how to adjust all the temperatures.

Cooking Language

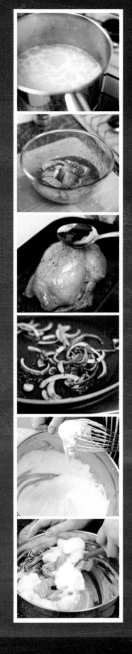

Simmering...
Means that the liquid in the pan is bubbling gently, 'boiling' and it's on a fast rumble. Usually, once food has come to the boil, it should be turned down to simmer. Boiling any food hard for a long time will not be good for the nutritional value or the taste.

Marinade...
Sounds a fancy word, but all it means is allowing food to soak over long periods of time in a mixture of oils, herbs spices etc.. It just enables the food to take on quite subtle flavours.

Basting...
When roasting larger pieces of meat or whole chickens recipes may ask you to 'baste' them. This simply means taking the roasting tin out of the oven, spooning out (using as big a spoon as is practical) the juices from the bottom of the pan and then pouring this over the top of the meat. This helps to keep the meat moist and returns the flavours back into the meat.

Browning (caramelizing)...
The reason we try to 'brown' certain foods when cooking is because, when we do this it adds extra flavour. For instance, when browning onions, natural sugars are released adding a lovely sweet flavour. This is why we call it 'caramelizing'.

Whisking/Whipping...
If you do not have an electric whisk you can use a large balloon whisk. It may take a little longer, but with some exercise is just as effective.
1. Place the food in a large metal bowl.

2. Tip the bowl on its side a little and use circular movements with the whisk. The idea of whisking is that you are incorporating air to increase the volume of a liquid.

Folding in...
is a gentle operation, use a metal spoon or silicon spatula.
1. Use slow even sweeps, mixing, first of all, around the sides of the bowl... ...then through the centre.

2. If you use quick movements, you will lose the 'air' or lightness from the mixture.

Roast a chicken

1. Preheat the oven to 180°C fan oven/200°C/ Gas 6. Wash the chicken and make sure it does not have any unwanted items in the cavity.

2. Place on a greased casserole dish or roasting tin. Spread a little oil over the chicken with your fingers. Add 1 mug of water. Sprinkle with salt and pepper.

3. Cover with a lid or foil. Place in the oven for 1 hour. Periodically baste with pan juices.

4. After 1 hour, take the lid or foil off and allow the chicken to brown. This timing is for a 2kg chicken. If you have a larger bird allow more time before taking off the foil, i.e. 3kg = 1½ hours, 4kg = 2 hours. In all cases take the foil off at the end to allow to brown, which should take about 30 to 45 minutes.

Pan roast chicken

1. Heat a little oil in a frying pan, add chicken breasts. Cook on a high heat for 2 minutes each side.

2. Turn down the heat and cook with the lid on for a further 4 minutes each side, depending on the size of the chicken breast.

3. Test by making a cut in the meat to see that it is no longer pink in the centre.

Cooking steak

1. Heat a little oil in a frying pan. Have the heat quite high and when the oil begins to have a heat haze above it, (it does not need to smoke) add the steaks.

2. How do you like your steaks?

3. The times below are for a 1" thick steak. If the steak is thinner, cook for less time.

RARE

2 MINS EACH SIDE High heat

2 MINS EACH SIDE Medium heat

MEDIUM

2 MINS EACH SIDE High heat

4 MINS EACH SIDE Medium heat

WELL DONE

2 MINS EACH SIDE High heat

6 MINS EACH SIDE Medium heat

Making croutons

1. Heat about 1 tablespoon of oil in a frying pan.

2. Using one thick slice of bread per person, dip the bread in the oil, allow it to absorb a little of the oil. Quickly turn it over and allow the other side to absorb the rest of the oil.

3. Fry over a medium heat for 1 minute, or until browned, turn over again and brown the other side.

4. Take out of the pan and cut into squares.

Poach an egg

1. Half fill a frying pan with water and bring to the boil. Turn down to simmer.

2. Break an egg into a mug or cup.

3. Gently tip the egg into the water. Allow the egg to cook gently; don't stir or turn the heat up.

4. After 4 - 5 minutes the egg should be cooked.

5. Using a slotted turner, gently lift the egg out and allow to drain.

6. Fresh eggs work the best, as old eggs will generally be difficult and spread all over the pan.

Melting chocolate

If you just put chocolate straight into a saucepan, the heat is too intense and often ruins the chocolate. You need to melt chocolate very slowly. Here is a proven method.

1. Put the chocolate in a bowl and place it over a pan of simmering water. Make sure that the water does not touch the bottom of the bowl.

2. Stir the chocolate every now and then.

3. Once it has melted, carefully take the bowl off the pan (the bowl will be hot) and leave to cool a little, before putting it in your recipe.

More than mash

'Mash' has had old-fashioned connotations for many years, but is making a definite comeback in modern cooking, rarely as 'simple mash'. Here are some ways to spice it up.

Basic mash for two

4 medium potatoes, peeled
2 x 1" cubes butter
salt and pepper

1. Cut the potatoes into 2" chunks.

2. Put the potatoes into boiling, salted water. Once the water has come back to the boil, turn down the heat, put a lid on the pan and cook for approximately 10 minutes.

3. Test after 10 minutes. If cooked, drain the water off. If not cooked, boil for a little longer taking care not to overcook or the potatoes will disintegrate into the water.

4. Add the butter and mash with a potato masher.

5. Mash until all the lumps have gone, but don't work the mash too much as it will become glutinous. Add salt and freshly ground pepper.

Cheddar and mustard mash

At the 'mashing stage', add ½ mug grated mature cheddar cheese, together with 1 good teaspoon of wholegrain mustard, salt and freshly ground black pepper. The wholegrain mustard also gives an attractive look to the mash.

Sweet potato mash

Just use half normal potatoes and half sweet potatoes.

Roast potatoes

45-50
MINS

180°C fan oven
200°C non-fan
Gas mark 6

1. Preheat the oven to 180°C fan oven/200°C/ Gas 6. Cut the potatoes into 2 - 3" chunks. You do not need to peel the potatoes.

2. Place them on a baking tray. Sprinkle with salt and oil. If you have some fresh rosemary, pull off the leaves and sprinkle over the potatoes (dried rosemary will also work fine).

3. Using your hands, make sure the oil is evenly distributed around the potatoes. Make sure that the potatoes are not flat side down, this will mean more of the potatoes will brown.

4. Cook in the oven for 45 - 50 minutes until they are brown.

Posh roast potatoes

1. Preheat the oven to 180°C fan oven/200°C/ Gas 6. Peel the potatoes. Cut into 2 - 3" chunks.

2. Place in a pan of boiling water and cook for 10 minutes.

3. Place a baking tray in the oven, with 2 tablespoons of vegetable oil in it.

4. Drain the potatoes and return to the pan. Put the lid on the pan and shake it quite vigorously. This will cause the outsides of the potatoes to become a little furry.

5. Place the potatoes on the heated baking tray and turn them, to distribute the oil. Put in the oven, for 45 - 50 minutes, until browned.

Mini roast potatoes

This a great way to make roast potatoes in a short time. They will cook in the time it takes to make the rest of a meal.

1. Preheat the oven to 180ºC fan oven/200ºC / Gas 6.

2. Cut the potatoes into 1" cubes. You don't need to peel them.

3. Place them on a baking tray, drizzle oil over them and season with salt and pepper. Mix the oil and seasoning into the potatoes with your hands.

4. Place in the oven, for 25 - 30 minutes, until browned.

5. You can sprinkle some dried rosemary over the potatoes if you wish.

Amazing wedges

1. Preheat the oven to 180ºC fan oven/200ºC/ Gas 6 . Cut the potatoes into wedges.

2. Place on baking trays and sprinkle with oil and salt. Distribute the oil well with your hands.

3. Make sure that each wedge is 'standing up', not sitting on a flat side. You will get nice and brown wedges this way and they won't stick to the tray as much.

4. Place in the oven for 25 - 30 minutes or until browned.

Perfect rice every time

To take the hassle out of making rice, simply remember these two things:

1. ½ a mug of rice per person.

2. Double the amount of water compared with rice.

Therefore for 2 people: 1 mug of rice + 2 mugs of water.

1. Bring the water to the boil.

2. If you are making pilau rice, add pilau rice seasoning to the water now. Stir briefly to distibute well.

3. Add the rice and turn the heat down to simmer gently. Do not stir.

4. Put the lid on and leave for 10 - 15 minutes. Check every now and then to see if the water has boiled away or not.

5. Once cooked, all the water should have gone and the rice should be light and fluffy. Basmati rice gives the best results.

Pasta

There are innumerable kinds of pasta to choose from in the shops, made from different ingredients. Most will have instructions on the packets as to how to cook them. Just in case you have lost the packet, here are some general guidelines:

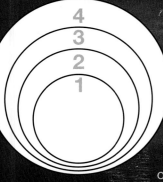

Spaghetti

Use the guide to the left for quantities per person. Boil sufficient water in a pan to cover the spaghetti whilst cooking. Once the water is boiling, lower the spaghetti sticks into the water. Once the half that is in the water has softened slightly, push the other half in. Take care not to get your fingers in the water! Simmer for 8 - 10 minutes. Test one piece to see if it is cooked. Drain the water off and add one teaspoon of butter or olive oil, mix around and this will stop the spaghetti sticking together.

Most other pastas

Again, boil enough water to cover the pasta. Once the water is boiling, add the pasta. One mug of dried pasta is plenty for one person with a very healthy appetite. Simmer for the appropriate time (see below), drain and add butter or olive oil to prevent the pasta sticking together.

Cooking times

Pasta is better slightly undercooked than overcooked (a little 'al dente', meaning best with a little crunch to it than all stuck together and soggy).

Below are the cooking times for various types of pasta:

1. Tagliatelle = 4-5 minutes
2. Spaghetti = 6 minutes
3. Radiatore = 10 minutes
4. Fusilli = 6-8 minutes
5. Penne = 10-12 minutes
6. Conchiglie = 6-8 minutes
7. Macaroni = 10-12 minutes
8. Farfalle = 6-8 minutes

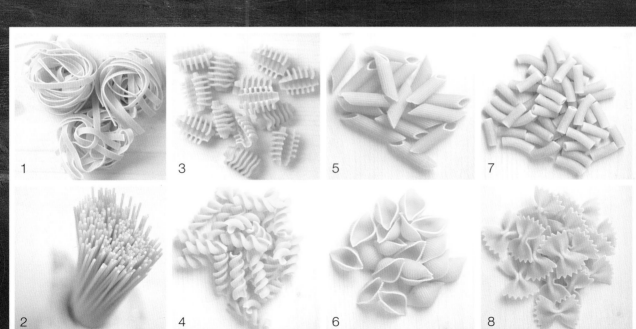

'Let's get cooking' secrets of success

Taste, Taste, Taste. One of the most important things about improving your cooking skills is to taste things as you cook. Once it's on the plate it's too late to make any changes apart from salt and pepper. For instance, if you think things are a little bland and you like stronger flavours, increase things like the amount of tomato purée, stock, salt and pepper or the herbs and spices in the recipe. Do this bit by bit and taste in between to see if you are going in the right direction. If things are a little bitter, then add a small amount of sugar. If it is too spicy, add lime or lemon juice and then write a note in the book to add less spice the next time you cook it. My recipe books at home are full of written notes.

Taste, change, experiment.

Improvise, but don't change things too radically or miss out essential ingredients. If it's in the title, it's essential.

Don't rush, it never saves any time, just makes you more stressed. Enjoy cooking. If you have guests leave plenty of time to prepare. If you are a bit late, and they are good friends, they won't mind.

For a calm, enjoyable cooking time, **gather together all your ingredients before you begin.** This way you won't be searching the kitchen for ingredients while your food is cooking on the hob. Make a clear space in your kitchen before you begin, even if you share the kitchen. Clean and chop all vegetables before you begin.

Read through the recipe before you begin to cook.

Plan your meals for the week. Sit down at the start of the week or before you go shopping and plan what you might want to eat that week, then simply shop according to what you need. It saves so much time and avoids having to return to the shops to get ingredients. Planning ahead means that you will only need to shop once or twice in a week and it avoids wasting food that you don't get round to using, as there is now a reason for everything being in your fridge.

Cooking enough to last a couple of days takes such a weight off your mind, when you come home from work on that second day and you know something is waiting for you in the fridge ready to simply heat up.

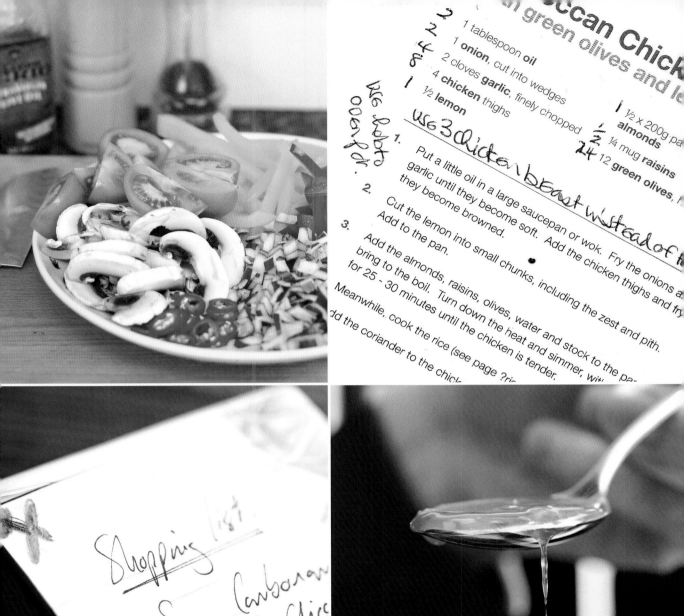

...ccan Chicken
...h green olives and le...

1 tablespoon **oil**
1 **onion**, cut into wedges
2 cloves **garlic**, finely chopped
4 **chicken** thighs
1 ½ **lemon**

1 ½ x 200g pa...
almonds
¼ mug **raisins**
12 **green olives**, ...

We 3 Chicken breast instead of th...

Use potato oven for.

1. Put a little oil in a large saucepan or wok. Fry the onions a... garlic until they become soft. Add the chicken thighs and fry... they become browned.

2. Cut the lemon into small chunks, including the zest and pith. Add to the pan.

3. Add the almonds, raisins, olives, water and stock to the pa... bring to the boil. Turn down the heat and simmer, wi... for 25 - 30 minutes until the chicken is tender.

Meanwhile, cook the rice (see page ?ri...

...dd the coriander to the chick...

Shopping list

Mea: Spag Carbonara...
...Poached Chic...
...Cut.
Tom S...

Tasty Snacks

Need a quick bite to eat but want something different from the same old sandwiches? Here are some great ideas for quick and easy snacks. Some are designed for ordinary days, others for more special occasions.

Often we only cook when other people are around and, if left to our own devices, we revert to the old beans on toast. Why not think about cooking being a treat not a chore and make these snacks just for yourself every now and then?

Roasted Tomato Soup
with fresh basil and crème fraîche

V £1.35 /PERSON EASE ★★ MAKES 4 PREP 15 MINS COOK 25 MINS

2 medium **potatoes,** cut into 1" cubes

6 **large tomatoes,** halved

1 tablespoon **olive oil**

1 **red onion,** sliced

2 cloves **garlic,** chopped

1 **vegetable stock cube** + 1½ mugs **water**

2 tablespoons **tomato purée**

2 dessertspoons **sugar**

2 tablespoons **crème fraîche** or **Greek yogurt**

2 tablespoons chopped **fresh basil**

salt and pepper

---

1. Put the oven on to heat at 200°C fan oven/220°C/Gas 7.

2. Place the potatoes and tomatoes on separate baking trays with the tomatoes placed cut side up. Sprinkle with olive oil and season well. Place in the oven for 25 minutes.

3. Heat a little oil in a large saucepan. Add the onions and garlic. Fry on a medium heat for 5 - 6 minutes until the onions soften and begin to brown.

4. Add the cooked tomatoes, potatoes, tomato purée, sugar, water and stock cube and cook for a further 3 - 4 minutes, stirring frequently.

5. Using a hand-held blender, blend the soup until you don't see any more lumps (unless you want it lumpy). Bring back to the boil. Stir in the basil, leaving a little behind to sprinkle on top when serving.

6. Serve in individual soup bowls. To make it look a little bit fancy, put a tablespoon of yogurt or crème fraîche in the middle of the soup; using a spoon handle swirl the yogurt or crème fraîche and sprinkle the leftover basil over the top. See photo.

NOTE: Tastier than anything you will buy in a tin and made from healthy fresh ingredients. Will freeze well if you have any leftovers.

Brie and Bacon Tartiflette
with crusty bread

3 large **potatoes**

250g pack of **pancetta** or **bacon lardons**

1 large **onion**, finely sliced

⅔ mug **water**

1 teaspoon **liquid chicken stock** or a **stock cube**

150g **Brie**

oil to fry

1. Preheat the oven to 200°C fan oven/ 220°C/Gas 7.

2. Slice the potatoes and boil for 10 minutes until just tender. Drain.

3. Heat some oil in a large pan and fry the lardons until they begin to brown. Set aside.

4. In the same pan, heat a little more oil and fry the onions until they also begin to brown.

5. With a little cooking oil, grease an ovenproof dish. Layer half of the potatoes on the bottom, then half the lardons and onions on top. Repeat with the rest of the ingredients.

6. Mix the water and stock together and pour over the ingredients in the dish.

7. Slice the Brie and place over the top.

8. Put in the oven for 20 minutes, the cheese should be a little brown.

9. Serve on its own or with crusty bread.

NOTE: This dish has it's origins in France. Apparently invented by the cheese manufacturers to boost their sales.

TIP: Fry the bacon lardons, until they are quite brown and crisp. This makes the dish more tasty.

WHERE ON EARTH:
Pancetta lardons are with the cooked meats, whereas the bacon lardons are usually with the rest of the bacon in the supermarket.

Butternut Soup
with Parmesan toast

1 dessert spoon **coriander seeds**

1 **onion**, sliced

1 **butternut squash** or **pumpkin** (approx 8 - 900g) peeled and cut into chunks

juice of ½ **lemon**

½ teaspoon **ground ginger**

1 teaspoon **cumin**

2 mugs **water**

1 **vegetable stock cube**, 1 tablespoon concentrated **liquid stock** or a **stock pot**

2 tablespoons **crème fraîche**

2 - 3 slices of **bread**

½ mug grated **Parmesan**

oil to fry

1. Toast the coriander seeds in a dry saucepan for 2 minutes on a high heat, shaking them frequently. Take care not to burn them. When they begin to crackle, take them off the heat and set aside in a small bowl until later.

2. In the same pan, heat some oil and fry the onions until the onions are golden brown, stirring frequently.

3. Add the pumpkin or butternut squash, ginger and cumin, fry for 1 - 2 minutes.

4. Add the water and stock and bring to the boil. Turn down the heat to simmer gently, with a lid on, for 5 - 10 minutes, or until the squash is tender.

5. While the soup is cooking, make the Parmesan toasts. Preheat the grill. Butter the bread and sprinkle the Parmesan over each slice of bread, toast until the Parmesan goes brown or begins to bubble.

6. Allow the soup to cool slightly and blitz with a hand-held blender. Add the lemon juice and crème fraîche.

7. Reheat the soup and serve.

NOTE: Pumpkin or butternut squash have a lovely sweet flavour and are yummy in this great looking soup. The Parmesan toasts are great to use with other soup recipes.

Quick and Easy Tuna Melts
with salad

2 or 3 **panini** or **ciabatta**

2 x 185g **tin tuna**, drained of oil

4 tablespoons **mayo**

½ teaspoon **cayenne pepper** or **paprika**

2 mugs grated **cheddar cheese**

salad to serve

chutney to serve (optional)

1. Preheat the grill.

2. Slice the bread horizontally, spread with butter.

3. In a bowl, mix the tuna, mayo and cayenne together. Don't mix too much as it will go mushy. Season with salt and pepper.

4. Spread mixture evenly over the breads. Generously sprinkle with cheese and then sprinkle a couple of pinches of paprika over each one.

5. Place under a hot grill for 5 minutes or until the cheese begins to brown.

6. Serve with green salad.

NOTE: A great and inexpensive way to use tinned tuna and turn it into a posh snack. The paprika gives a little zing to the melts.

Mozzarella and Tomato Puff Pastry Tart
with salad

2 sheets uncooked, defrosted **puff pastry**

2 **red onions**, sliced into thin wedges

400g pack of **mozzarella** cheese

5 - 6 large **tomatoes**, thickly sliced

1 tablespoon chopped **fresh basil**

salt and **pepper**

oil for frying

salad to serve

---

1. Preheat the oven to 220°C fan oven/220°C/Gas 7.

2. Place the sheets of pastry on baking trays. Using the point of a sharp knife, make a line about half an inch in from the edge of the pastry, creating a border. Using a fork, prick the centre part with lots of holes, making sure you don't touch your bordered area. This ensures that only the border will rise when you put it in the oven.

3. Bake for 15 minutes in the oven.

4. While the pastry is cooking, fry the onions in a little olive oil, for approximately 1 - 2 minutes, until they become soft.

5. Slice the mozzarella.

6. After 15 minutes in the oven, the pastry should be golden brown. Remove from the oven. If the pastry has risen in the centre, gently push down with the back of a fork.

7. Arrange the ingredients evenly on the pastry, starting with the onions, followed by the tomatoes, with the cheese on the top. Season well with freshly ground black pepper and return to the oven for 10 minutes.

8. When the tart is cooked, sprinkle the basil over the top. If you chose to use dried basil, sprinkle over the top before the tart goes back into the oven.

9. Serve with green salad.

NOTE: Very simple to cook, makes a tasty snack, great for a weekend snack when friends are round. You can use different, stronger cheeses if you wish.

TIP: It is very useful to keep a packet of frozen puff pastry in the freezer. It will defrost in 1 hour, making a very useful stand-by.

Posh Cheese on Toast
with balsamic dressing

1. Cut the bread in 2 horizontally. Lightly toast both sides under a grill.

2. Butter the toasted bread. Sprinkle the onions, olives and tomatoes evenly over the bread.

3. Cut the cheese into strips and place over the top.

4. Place back under the hot grill for 5 - 6 minutes or until the cheese begins to bubble.

5. Mix together the vinegar and oil in a small bowl or mug and drizzle over the hot toasts.

6. Serve with a little Bistro salad.

2 **ciabatta, bagel or panini**

a little **butter**

4 **spring onions**, sliced thinly lengthways

10 **olives**, chopped

6 **tomatoes**, sliced

250g **Camembert** or other kind of soft cheese

1 dessertspoon **balsamic vinegar**

1 dessertspoon **olive oil**

1 bag **bistro salad**

NOTE: Simple to make, not too expensive and gives a tasty twist to boring cheese on toast.

WHERE ON EARTH: Balsamic vinegar is usually found over the freezers, near the pickles or with the oils.

Do It Yourself Panini
with salad

£1.35 /PERSON   EASE ★   SERVES 3   PREP 15 MINS

1. Cut the panini horizontally.

2. Spread with butter and fill with the ham, tomato and slices of cheese.

3. Heat a frying pan, do not add oil. Turn down to a medium heat.

4. Place the panini in the pan and place another saucepan on top (make sure the bottom is clean). Put some kind of heavy weight in the pan that won't melt, enough weight to squash the panini down a bit.

5. Cook for 2 minutes, remove the pan and turn over the panini, then return the pan with weight. Cook for a further 2 minutes.

6. Serve with some green salad.

2 **panini**

4 slices of **ham**

2 **tomatoes**, cut into thick slices

Cheddar cheese, sliced thinly

NOTE: Here's a way to make your own toasted panini without an expensive press. You can of course vary the fillings, for instance, using any cooked meat from the deli section at the supermarket, tuna, cooked chicken etc.

More than Just Salads

Tired of boring lettuce, tomatoes and cucumber? Salads can be so much more. They are not just something that goes with a "proper meal". These are scrumptious and complete meals in themselves. I have included some traditional ones, like Ceasar salad, and some more unusual ones, like the Indonesian salad. Fresh ingredients are the key to great tasting salads.

Sweet and Spicy Chicken Rice
with salad

1 mug **rice**

1 teaspoon **pilau rice seasoning**

2 **chicken breasts**

3 tablespoons **korma curry paste**

1 green **eating apple**

1 small tin **sweetcorn**

⅓ mug **raisins**

4 **spring onions**, chopped

6 tablespoons **mayo**

oil to fry

green salad to serve

1. Make the pilau rice (see page 22). Once cooked, take off the heat and allow to cool.

2. Pan roast the chicken (see page 16). Set aside on a plate and allow the chicken to cool.

3. Add the curry paste to the pan used for the chicken and cook for 30 seconds, then allow to cool.

4. Cut the unpeeled apple into chunks (removing the core). Place in a bowl with the sweetcorn, raisins, cooled rice and spring onions.

5. Cut the cooled chicken into chunks, add to the bowl and mix.

6. Combine the mayo and curry paste, pour over the rest of the ingredients in the bowl and mix.

7. Serve with green salad.

NOTE: Keeps well in the fridge until the next day and makes a great summer salad.

TIP: Be sure to keep this salad in the fridge as soon as it is cool. You need to take care with rice, as it can breed toxins when left at room temperature for long periods.

Classic Ceasar Salad
with mustard dressing

2 **chicken breasts**

2 slices of **wholemeal bread**

1 **Cos lettuce** or hearts of **Romaine lettuce**

½ **cucumber**, cut into chunks

6 **anchovies**

6 **spring onions**, chopped

oil to fry

Parmesan to serve

Dressing

2 tablespoons **mayo**

1 tablespoon **olive oil**

juice of a **lemon**

1 dessertspoon **wholegrain mustard**

1. Pan roast the chicken (see page 16). Set aside on a plate and allow the chicken to cool while you prepare the rest of the ingredients.

2. Make the croutons (see page 17). Leave to cool.

3. Cut the lettuce into bite-size pieces, place in a bowl with the cucumber, chopped anchovies and spring onions. Mix together and divide between the appropriate number of plates.

4. Sprinkle the croutons over the top of the salad.

5. Slice the chicken breasts and arrange over the salad.

6. Mix all the dressing ingredients well and drizzle over the top.

7. Shave the Parmesan using a potato peeler; it should produce shavings of Parmesan. Sprinkle over the top of the salad.

NOTE: This is an absolutely classic salad. Well worth learning how to make.

WHERE ON EARTH:
Anchovy fillets are sold in small jars and usually found with the tinned meats and fish. Olives are usually near the freezers and the pickles.

| £1.90 /PERSON | EASE ★★ | SERVES 2 | PREP 15 MINS |

Greek Tuna and Black Olive Salad
with mustard dressing

½ x pack **bistro salad**

¼ **cucumber**, cut into chunks

4 **spring onions**

12 **olives**, cut into pieces

3 **tomatoes**, cut into wedges

200g tin **tuna** in oil, drained of oil

salt and **pepper**

Fresh crusty **bread** or **ciabatta** to serve.

Dressing

2 tablespoons **mayo**

1 tablespoon **olive oil**

juice of a **lemon**

1 dessertspoon **wholegrain mustard**

1. Put enough bistro salad for 2 people into a mixing bowl.

2. Add the cucumber, onions, olives and tomatoes.

3. Tip the tuna out of the tin into a small bowl and break up into pieces. Add to the salad and gently mix all the ingredients together. Divide between the 2 plates.

4. Mix all the dressing ingredients together and drizzle over the salads.

5. Serve with crusty bread or ciabatta.

NOTE: We all think of tuna as a basic ingredient. If it is mixed with ingredients that complement it, then its flavour can be delicious.

Chicken, Feta and Avocado Salad
with lemon dressing

1 **chicken breast**

½ x 140g pack of **bistro salad**

1 tablespoon freshly chopped **mint**

10 - 12 **cherry tomatoes**, halved

2 **spring onions**, chopped

10 **black olives**, sliced in half

1 ripe **avocado**

½ x 200g pack of **feta cheese**

Dressing

juice of half a **lemon**

2 tablespoons **olive oil**

1 teaspoon **sugar**

salt and **pepper**

1. Pan roast the chicken (see page 16). Set aside on a plate and allow the chicken to cool a little while you prepare the rest of the ingredients.

2. Mix together the bistro salad, mint, tomatoes, spring onions and olives.

3. Peel the avocado and cut into bite-size pieces. Add to the salad.

4. Cut the feta into cubes and add to the salad. Arrange on the plates.

5. The chicken should be cool enough to slice and then arrange over the top of each plate.

6. Mix all the dressing ingredients in a mug or small bowl and drizzle over the salad.

NOTE: A lovely fresh salad with a Mediterranean flavour. Almost makes you think you were there! Great for a summers day.

TIP: The best way to peel an avocado is to cut the unpeeled fruit into ¼'s lengthways. Put the knife in the cuts and ease the fruit off the stone. Take each ¼ and ease your thumb under the top edge of the skin and gently peel off.

Indonesian Salad
with crunchy peanut and soy dressing

2 **eggs**

3 - 4 medium sized **new potatoes**, cut into bite-size pieces

1 medium **carrot**, quartered lengthways and cut into 2" sticks

½ small **broccoli** head, cut into small florets

10 - 12 **green beans**, cut in half

2 **spring onions**, cut into small rings

¼ x 400g pack of **bean sprouts**

green salad

Dressing

2 tablespoons crunchy **peanut butter**

1 small clove **garlic**, chopped finely

juice of 1 **lemon**

3 **anchovies**, chopped

1 tablespoon dark **soy sauce**

1 tablespoon **sugar**

1 tablespoon **water**

1. Put the eggs into boiling water and boil gently for 12 minutes. Drain the boiling water off and run under cold water. Peel the eggs and cut into quarters lengthways.

2. Place the potatoes in boiling water and simmer for 5 minutes.

3. Add the carrots and simmer for a further 5 minutes.

4. Add the broccoli and the green beans and simmer for another 5 minutes until the broccoli is tender.

5. Strain off the hot water and run the vegetables under cold water for 30 seconds. Drain and mix in with the spring onions and bean sprouts.

6. Mix all the dressing ingredients in a bowl.

7. Put a little green salad on each plate and then pile up the vegetable mix, putting the eggs on top. Drizzle a little of the dressing over. Serve the rest of the dressing in individual small bowls.

NOTE: An unusual, flavoursome salad. The peanut dressing can be used with other salads.

TIP: When hard-boiling eggs, cool them as quickly as possible by running under cold water. This stops the edges of the yolk from going black.

Bacon and Crouton Pancake Turnover
with honey and lemon dressing

Croutons

2 tablespoons **olive oil**

2 slices of **wholemeal bread**

Dressing

juice of a **lemon**

2 tablespoons thick **honey**

salt and **pepper**

Filling

½ **red pepper**, cut into long thin strips

1 **little gem lettuce**, cut into strips

2" **cucumber**, cut into long strips

2 sticks of **celery**, sliced

2 **spring onions**, cut into long strips

6 rashers of **streaky bacon**, crispy fried and cut into chunks

Pancakes

3 **eggs**

2 tablespoons **flour**

2 tablespoons **water**

salt and **pepper**

1. Heat the 2 tablespoons of oil in a frying pan. Quickly dip each side of the bread in the oil and fry until browned. Take out of the pan and cut into long thin strips.

2. Mix the dressing ingredients together in a bowl.

3. Combine the filling ingredients together in a mixing bowl, along with the croutons.

4. In a separate large bowl beat together the eggs, flour, water and salt and pepper, making sure there are no lumps.

5. Heat a little oil in a frying pan and pour in ⅓ of the pancake mixture, tip the pan so the egg is evenly spread. Cook for 1 minute, lifting the edge to check that the bottom has browned slightly. With a fish slice turn the pancake over and cook on the other side for 1 minute. Repeat with the other 2 pancakes.

6. Put a pancake on each plate and share the filling ingredients between them. Pour over the dressing and fold the pancake over (see photo).

NOTE: This salad has lots of different, complementary textures and flavours. The honey and lemon dressing is delightful with the bacon.

Oriental Marinated Chicken Strips
with bistro salad

Marinade

1 teaspoon **oil**

1 clove **garlic**, chopped finely

1 tablespoon **hoisin sauce**

1 teaspoon **soy sauce**

juice of ½ **lime**

1 teaspoon **ground cumin**

½ fat **red chilli**, deseeded and cut into rings

1 **chicken breast,** cut into thin strips

1 tablespoon **oil**

1 bag **bistro salad**

Salad dressing

1 tablespoon **olive oil**

juice of 1 **lime**

2 teaspoons **sugar**

1 tablespoon chopped **fresh coriander leaves**

1. Mix the marinade ingredients together in a bowl. Add the chicken and leave overnight in the fridge. If you do not have time to do this, 1 hour will be OK.

2. Mix the salad dressing in a small bowl or mug and set to one side until needed.

3. Heat a little oil in a wok. Take the chicken pieces from the marinade and stir fry on high heat for 2 - 3 minutes. The chicken will cook quite quickly as it is in small pieces.

4. Divide the salad between the plates. Sprinkle the dressing over and serve the chicken on the top of the salad.

NOTE: After marinading the chicken overnight, this becomes great fast food. Interesting fusion of East and West in the taste of this recipe.

WHERE ON EARTH:
Hoisin sauce is found in the 'world food' section at the supermarket.

Fast Food

You may have a little bit more money than when you were a student, but you will probably have less time. Here are some ideas for fast meals, taking between 15 minutes to half an hour to prepare, so easy to do when you get home from work. Keep some of the basic ingredients, such as rice and pasta, in the storecupboard, chicken breasts, some pieces of fish or prawns in the freezer. Decide each morning, before you leave for work, what needs to come out of the freezer and things will be easy when you come to cook in the evening.

Hoisin Chicken Noodles
with ginger and garlic

3 **spring onions**, sliced

1 teaspoon grated fresh **ginger**

1 clove **garlic**, finely chopped

1 **chicken breast**, cut into thin strips

3 **mushrooms**, sliced

1½ mugs boiling **water**

1 teaspoon **concentrated chicken stock**

1 teaspoon **soy sauce**

2 tablespoons **hoisin sauce**

½ x 340g can **sweetcorn**

½ x 400g pack of **fresh egg noodles** or **straight-to-wok noodles**

1 tablespoon **oil**

1. Heat the oil in a wok. Add the onions, ginger and garlic. Fry for 30 seconds.

2. Add the chicken to the wok and stir fry for 1 minute.

3. Add the mushrooms and stir fry for 30 seconds.

4. Add the water, stock, soy, hoisin, sweetcorn and noodles. Bring to the boil, then turn down to simmer for 1 minute.

5. Season well and serve in individual bowls.

NOTE: Really delicious fast food. As this recipe only uses one chicken breast to serve two people, it is also a money saver.

WHERE ON EARTH:
You can find fresh egg noodles and bean sprouts in the 'fresh veg' area of the supermarket. Hoisin sauce is usually with the 'world foods' and curry pastes.

Poached Chicken
with chilli sauce

2 **chicken breasts**

1 mug **water**

pinch of **salt**

2 mugs **water**

1 teaspoon **pilau rice seasoning**

1 mug **basmati rice**

Sauce

1 tablespoon **oil**

4 **spring onions**, cut into thin slices

2 teaspoon grated **fresh ginger**

2 cloves **garlic**, finely chopped

¼ fat **red chilli**, thinly sliced

juice of 2 **limes**

2 teaspoon **soy sauce**

2 tablespoon **hoisin sauce**

1 **cucumber**, cut into thin strips with a vegetable peeler, see photo.

1. Put the mug of water into a saucepan, add a pinch of salt and bring to the boil. Once boiling, add the chicken breast. Simmer gently for 2 - 3 minutes with the lid on the pan. Take off the heat and leave to stand for 15 minutes.

2. Make the pilau rice (see page 22). Once cooked, set aside with the lid on.

3. To make the sauce, heat the oil in a frying pan, add the onion, ginger and garlic and fry for 30 seconds. Add the rest of the sauce ingredients and bring to the boil. Once the sauce has boiled, turn off the heat and set aside until needed.

4. When the chicken is cooked, take out of the water and cut into slices.

5. Arrange the slices on a bed of rice. Put the cucumber strips alongside and pour some of the sauce over the chicken. Serve the rest of the sauce in a small bowl.

NOTE: Poaching chicken is a very simple, healthy way of cooking, and leaves the meat succulently tender and moist. If you like things very spicy just add more of the fresh chilli.

TIP: Always wash your hands well immediately after handling chillies. Be careful not to touch or rub your eyes while handling them.

£2.35 /PERSON   EASE ★★★   SERVES 2   PREP 25 MINS

Curried Chicken Breast
with a Greek yogurt sauce

1 mug **rice**

mangetout, cut into thin strips

oil to fry

1 **onion**, cut into thin slices

2 **chicken breasts**

1 tablespoon **korma curry paste**

½ mug **water**

1 teaspoon **liquid chicken stock** or ½ a **stock cube**

1 tablespoon **tomato purée**

1 teaspoon **sugar**

Sauce

2 tablespoon **Greek yogurt**

juice of ½ **lemon**

1 tablespoon chopped **fresh coriander leaves**

---

1. Make the rice (see page 22). At the end of the cooking time, turn off the heat and put the mangetout in the pan, replace the lid and leave for a few minutes. The mangetout will cook in the heat of the pan.

2. Meanwhile, heat the oil in a frying pan. Add the onions, fry for 1 - 2 minutes until they begin to soften. Add the chicken and cook for 1 minute each side on high heat. Stir the onions while the chicken is cooking.

3. Add the curry paste and cook for about 30 seconds.

4. Add the stock and water, tomato purée and sugar, bring to the boil. Turn down to simmer, with a lid on the pan, for 8 - 10 minutes until the chicken is cooked.

5. By now the rice and mangetout should be cooked.

6. Mix together the yogurt, lemon juice and coriander.

7. Serve the chicken on top of the rice and mangetout and spoon the juices from the pan over the chicken. Serve the yogurt sauce at the side.

NOTE: Yogurt and curry are a wonderful, classic combination. The chicken is cooked in the curry sauce, keeping it moist and tender.

TIP: Cooking the vegetables in the same pan as the rice is quite efficient. You can do this with frozen peas, mangetout, sugar snaps or courgettes. The courgettes would need to be chopped quite small, but will still cook in 2 - 3 minutes.

Pan Roast Chicken Breast
with mustard sauce

Salad dressing

1 tablespoon **olive oil**

1 tablespoon **balsamic vinegar**

1 teaspoon **sugar**

salt and **pepper**

Mustard Sauce

2 tablespoons **crème fraîche** or **soured cream**

1 tablespoon **wholegrain mustard**

12 - 14 new **potatoes**

2 **chicken breasts**

salad

1. Put the water on to boil. Once boiling, add the potatoes and cook for 10 - 15 minutes until they are tender. Drain, return to the pan, put a lid on and leave until required.

2. Make the salad dressing by mixing the ingredients together. If possible put the ingredients in a jar and shake, otherwise stir well in a bowl.

3. Make the sauce by mixing the crème fraîche and mustard together in another bowl.

4. Pan roast the chicken (see page 16). Remove from the pan and slice, see photo.

5. Serve with the salad, dressing, potatoes and sauce.

NOTE: Frying and oven-baking chicken breast can cause them to become dry. This method of cooking keeps them moist and tender.

TIP: This is more of a basic recipe and is versatile. You can serve the chicken with potato wedges, mini roasts (see Cook School), and many different salads.

WHERE ON EARTH:
Balsamic vinegar is usually found over the freezers, near the pickles.

Chicken and Cashew Hoisin Stir Fry
with fresh egg noodles

£2.40 /PERSON   EASE ★   SERVES 2-3   PREP 25 MINS

1 **onion**, cut into thin wedges

1 **garlic** clove, chopped finely

½ **red pepper,** cut into thin strips

1 pack of **sweetcorn** and **mangetout**, sliced lengthways

2 **chicken breasts**, cut into bite-size pieces

1 pack of **fresh egg noodles**

½ x 100g pack of **unsalted cashew nuts**

1 tablespoon **oil**

Sauce

½ mug **water** + 1 teaspoon **liquid chicken stock** or ½ **stock cube**

3 tablespoons **hoisin sauce**

1 teaspoon **sugar**

1. Heat the oil in a wok. Add the onions, garlic and peppers, fry for a minute.

2. Add the chicken and sweetcorn. Keep the heat high, stir frequently and cook until the chicken is no longer pink.

3. Add the mangetout, stir for 30 seconds.

4. Mix together the sauce ingredients, add to the wok and bring to the boil.

5. Once the liquid is boiling, turn the heat down and simmer with a lid on the wok for a minute.

6. Add the noodles and cashews and cook for another minute. Mix well and serve.

NOTE: Lots of yummy tastes and different textures in this classic stir fry.

TIP: You can make this meal cheaper by using dried or ready-to-wok egg noodles.

WHERE ON EARTH: Cashew nuts are in the baking section with the dried fruits. Hoisin sauce will be found with the 'world foods' and curry pastes.

Chicken and Mushroom Pasta
with 'Philly' cheese and fresh basil

¼ x 500g pack **Tagliatelle** or one mug pasta

1 small **onion**, sliced

1 clove **garlic**, finely chopped

1 **chicken breast**, cut into thin strips

6 **mushrooms**, sliced

½ x 200g packet of **Philadelphia soft cheese**

1 tablespoon chopped **fresh basil**

salt and **pepper**

2 tablespoons coarsely grated **Parmesan cheese**

oil to fry

1. Cook the pasta (see page 23). Once cooked, drain, return to the pan and add a little olive oil to prevent sticking. Replace lid to keep warm.

2. As the pasta is cooking, heat a little oil in a frying pan. Fry the onions and garlic for 2 - 3 minutes until the onions begin to soften.

3. Add the chicken and cook until the chicken is no longer pink.

4. Add the mushrooms, cook for 1 minute. Take off the heat and add the cream cheese and the herbs and stir until the cheese has melted. Stir into the pasta. Taste and season.

5. Sprinkle the Parmesan on top.

NOTE: Delightful mix of chicken and cheeses. One chicken breast easily makes enough for two people , so saves a few pennies.

TIP: Keep your block of Parmesan in a resealable bag in the fridge and it will keep for months.

Rump Steak
with Lebanese style couscous

£3.50 /PERSON   EASE ★★★   SERVES 2   PREP 30 MINS

1 mug boiling **water** from kettle +
1 teaspoon **liquid beef stock**

1 mug **couscous**

1 teaspoon **cumin**

6 **spring onions**, chopped

3 - 4 mugs thinly sliced **apricots**

1 tablespoon chopped **fresh mint**

1 tablespoon chopped **fresh basil**

1 x ¾" thick piece of **rump steak**

12 **cherry tomatoes**, cut in half

½ mug **pine nuts**

Dressing

1 tablespoon **olive oil**

1 tablespoon **white wine vinegar**

1 teaspoon **sugar**

salt and **pepper**

---

1. Add the water and stock to the couscous in a bowl. Stir and cover. Leave to stand for about 5 minutes. Fluff up with a fork and add the cumin, spring onions, apricots, mint and basil.

2. While the couscous is soaking, mix together the dressing ingredients.

3. Cook the steak (see page 17). Once cooked, take the steak out of the pan and leave to rest.

4. Fry the pine nuts in the steak juices left in the pan for 1 minute. Add the pine nuts to the dressing.

5. Add the tomatoes to the couscous salad and stir. Divide between the 2 plates.

6. Cut the steak into thin slices and arrange over the top of the couscous. Drizzle the dressing over the top.

NOTE: An unusual meaty, sweet and spicy couscous dish, with Eastern flavours.

TIP: Although rump steak is more expensive, a little goes a long way in this dish. Any leftovers can be eaten cold. Don't try to reheat, as the meat will be tough if you microwave it.

WHERE ON EARTH: Ready-to-eat apricots and pine nuts are in the baking section with dried fruits.

Beef Chow Mein
with oyster sauce

Sauce

1 tablespoon grated **fresh ginger**

1 clove **garlic**, finely chopped

1 tablespoon **tomato purée**

3 tablespoons **oyster sauce**

2 tablespoons **soy sauce**

½ mug **water**

Noodles

1 **onion**, thinly sliced

1 **red pepper**, cut into slices

1 x 350g piece **rump steak**, cut into thin slices

½ x 400g bag **bean sprouts**

385g packet **egg noodles**

oil to fry

1. Mix the sauce ingredients together in a bowl.

2. Heat a little oil in a wok. Add the onions and peppers and cook on a high heat until they become slightly soft.

3. Add the beef and cook until it is no longer pink.

4. Add the sauce and cook until it bubbles.

5. Add the bean sprouts and noodles. Cook for 1 minute or until everything is heated through.

6. Serve in bowls.

NOTE: Quick to make and a fraction of the cost of a takeaway. The sauce is lovely and yummy.

TIP: You will need to use good steak for this recipe, as it has to be cooked quickly. A little will go a long way when cut up thinly, so don't worry too much about the price.

WHERE ON EARTH: Oyster Sauce is found in the 'world food' section of the supermarket. The fresh beansprouts and noodles are near the fresh veg/salad section.

Pork with Homemade Apple Chutney
and pilau rice

Sauce

1 **onion**, chopped

1 clove **garlic**, finely chopped

1 **Granny Smith apple**, cored and roughly chopped

1 **lemon**, **juice** and **rind**

1 tablespoon **soy sauce**

1½ tablespoons **honey**

2 teaspoons **pilau rice seasoning**

1 mug **rice**

½ x 200g pack **mangetout**, cut into strips

2 **pork steaks**

1. To make the sauce, heat a little oil in a small saucepan, add the onions and garlic and fry until they begin to turn golden brown. Add the apples and cook for 1 minute. Add the lemon juice, rind, soy sauce, honey and 2 tablespoons water. Bring to the boil and cook for 1 - 2 minutes. Set to one side until the rest of the meal is cooked. You can reheat when the pork steak is cooked.

2. Make the pilau rice (see page 22). Once cooked, leave to stand with the lid on.

3. Once the rice is cooked, add the mangetout to the pan. Replace the lid and it will cook sufficiently in the heat from the pan. You do not need to put back on the heat.

4. Heat a little oil in a frying pan. Add the pork steaks. Cook on a high heat for 2 minutes each side. Turn the heat down, put a lid on the pan and cook for a further 4 minutes each side. This timing is for a steak that is approximately 1" thick. Just make a cut into one of the steaks to check it is cooked thoroughly. Pork steaks should not be 'bloody', but can still look a little pink inside.

5. Stir the mangetout into the rice. Serve the steak on top of the rice and pour the sauce over the top. See photo.

NOTE: Pork and apple, classic and delicious but with a little Eastern twist.

TIP: If you want the rice to look a little posh, as in the photo, you can buy a metal ring, or make one by cutting a section out of the middle of a large plastic drinks bottle (a bit Blue Peterish but it works just as well). Then you just form the rice in the ring and remove to leave a lovely tower of rice that rarely fails to impress.

TIP: If the steaks you are using are thinner (½" thick), it could be sufficiently cooked after the first 2 minutes each side.

Traditional Pork Steaks
with honey and mustard sauce

12 - 14 **new potatoes**

4 **carrots**, cut into sticks

2 **pork steaks**

1 x 200g pack **green beans**

Sauce

1 **onion**, finely chopped

1½ tablespoons grated **ginger**

½ teaspoon **cumin**

¼ teaspoon **cinnamon**

1 teaspoon **flour**

1 tablespoon **honey**

1 dessertspoon **wholegrain mustard**

⅓ mug **water**

salt and **pepper**

oil to fry

1. Put the water on to boil ready for the vegetables. Simmer the potatoes and carrots for 10 - 15 minutes or until tender. After 10 minutes, put the beans into the same pan.

2. Heat a little oil in a small saucepan and fry the onions until they begin to brown.

3. Add the ginger, cumin and cinnamon and fry for 30 seconds.

4. Add the flour and stir well. Cook for 30 seconds.

5. Add the rest of the sauce ingredients and bring to the boil. Simmer for 2 minutes Taste and season appropriately. If you want, you can blitz this sauce with a hand-held blender.

6. While the vegetables are cooking, heat a little oil in a frying pan. Add the pork steaks. Cook on a high heat for 2 minutes each side. Turn the heat down, put a lid on the pan and cook for a further 3 - 4 minutes each side. This timing is for a steak that is approximately 1" thick. If the steak is ½" thick, it could be cooked after the first 2 minutes each side. Just make a cut into one of the steaks to check. Pork steaks should not be 'bloody', but can still look quite pink inside.

7. Drain the vegetables and serve with the steaks and the sauce. You may need to reheat the sauce at the last minute.

NOTE: Wonderful, tender pork steaks, served with a sweet sauce and fresh vegetables. Great one to do when mum and dad come to visit, will really impress!

TIP: Pork should not be eaten when the meat is 'pink in the middle'. Pork in itself is 'pink', so if you gently press the steaks and blood comes out, it is not properly cooked. If you follow the timings in the recipe with a timer, it should be OK.

Chorizo Spaghetti
with balsamic and basil sauce

spaghetti (for amount see page 22)

1 **onion**, chopped

1 clove **garlic**, finely chopped

½ **red pepper**, chopped

4 small **chorizo sausages**, cut into small pieces

2 **tomatoes**, cut into 6 chunks

12 **olives**, halved

1 tablespoon chopped **fresh basil**

oil to fry

Sauce

1 tablespoon **balsamic vinegar**

2 tablespoons **red wine vinegar**

2 tablespoons **sugar**

1. Cook the spaghetti (see page 22). Drain and return to the pan, add a little olive oil, stir and leave in the pan with the lid on.

2. While the spaghetti is cooking, heat a little oil in a frying pan. Add the chorizo and fry for 1 - 2 minutes until cooked. Remove from the pan and set to one side.

3. Add the onion, garlic and peppers to the pan and fry for 2 - 3 minutes.

4. Add the sauce ingredients to the pan and cook until it begins to thicken slightly, approximately 3 - 4 minutes.

5. Add the chorizo, tomatoes and olives to the pan and cook for 1 minute.

6. Serve over the spaghetti. Sprinkle the basil over each serving.

NOTE: Chorizo are Spanish in origin and are spicy pork sausages. They are very much in fashion at the moment. They go well here with the balsamic dressing.

WHERE ON EARTH: Chorizo sausages are often at the deli counter, sometimes near the normal sausages. Olives are found near the pickles, usually over the freezers.

Quick and Easy Spaghetti Carbonara
with Parmesan

½ x 500g pack **spaghetti**

1 **onion**, thinly sliced

1 clove **garlic**

200g pack **pancetta lardons** or strips of **streaky bacon**

1 tablespoon **olive oil**

2 **eggs**

a little freshly grated **Parmesan**

1 tablespoon chopped **fresh basil**

1. Put the spaghetti on to cook (see page 22).

2. Heat a little oil in a wok and fry the onions and garlic until the onions are soft. Add the pancetta lardons and cook until they begin to brown.

3. Put the eggs in a large bowl and beat well.

4. Drain the pasta, but retain a little of the cooking liquid (about 2 tablespoons).

5. Stir all the ingredients, except the basil, into the bowl containing the beaten egg. The heat from the spaghetti and the lardons should cook the eggs and create a creamy sauce.

6. Add the chopped basil.

NOTE: Quick and easy to do. Classic Italian dish.

TIP: Pancetta lardons are not expensive and will keep in the fridge for a couple of weeks if they are not opened.

WHERE ON EARTH: The pancetta lardons are with the cooked meats and sliced pancetta. Bacon lardons are with the bacon.

Thai Prawn Curry
with rice

1 mug **rice**

pilau rice seasoning

1 x 180g pack of **cooked prawns**

1 tablespoon **oil**

1½ tablespoons **Thai red curry paste**

½ x 400g tin **coconut milk**

200g pack of **mangetout** and **baby sweetcorn**, both cut in half lengthways

6 spring **onions**, chopped

1. Make the pilau rice (see page 22).

2. Place the prawns on some kitchen paper to absorb any extra moisture from them.

3. Heat the oil in a frying pan. Add the curry paste and cook for 30 seconds, stirring frequently. Add the coconut milk and baby sweetcorn. Cook on a high heat for 3 - 4 minutes, the sauce should thicken slightly.

4. Add the prawns, spring onions, and mangetout to the curry and cook for 1 - 2 minutes.

5. When the rice is cooked, serve the curry on top of the rice.

NOTE: This is a lovely fresh, sweet, delicate curry. The crunchy vegetables make a great complement.

TIP: Be careful not to overcook the prawns, as they will become rubbery.

WHERE ON EARTH: Coconut milk is near the 'world foods', noodles and sauces.

Crispy Parmesan Fish
with fresh tomato sauce and mini roasts

Tomato and Basil Sauce

oil to fry

1 **onion**, sliced

1 x 400g **tin tomatoes**

1 teaspoon freshly ground **black pepper**

1 tablespoon **tomato purée**

1 tablespoon white **wine vinegar**

1 teaspoon **sugar**

2 tablespoon **fresh basil**, chopped

1 mug fresh **breadcrumbs**

1 mug grated **Parmesan**

juice and zest of a **lemon**

3 medium **potatoes**

2 pieces of **cod**, or **haddock**, cut into 2" strips

1 **egg**, beaten

2 tablespoons **olive oil**

---

1. Preheat the oven to 200°C fan oven/220°C/Gas 7.

2. Make the tomato sauce. Heat a little oil in a small saucepan, fry the onions until they become soft. Add the rest of the ingredients, apart from the basil, and cook for 2 - 4 minutes. Blitz with a hand-held blender. Add the basil and set aside until needed.

3. Make the breadcrumb mix. You can make breadcrumbs with a hand-held blender or simply rub the bread between your fingers. Mix the breadcrumbs with the Parmesan, lemon zest and juice and season well with salt and pepper.

4. Make the mini roasts (see page 21).

5. Prepare the fish. Grease a baking tray or ovenproof dish. Put the fish in a bowl with the egg, coat each piece of fish with the egg. Remove from the egg mixture and dip the fish in the breadcrumbs, attaching as much as possible to the fish. Put the fish on a greased baking tray or casserole dish. Place in the oven 10 minutes before the end of the cooking time for the potatoes.

6. If necessary, reheat the sauce and serve with the fish and potatoes.

NOTE: Wonderful, light, fresh tasting dish. The lemon and Parmesan in the crust is subtle and delightful.

TIP: You can use the tomato and basil sauce with other dishes. Any leftover sauce can be used with pasta the next day.

Zesty Tuna Steaks
with chilli tagliatelle

3 'bunches' or ⅕ x 500g pack of **tagliatelle** per person

olive oil to fry

6 **spring onions**, chopped

1 fat **red chilli**, deseeded and cut into thin rings

2 **tuna steaks**, cut into 1" square pieces

15 **black olives**

1 dessertspoon **fresh thyme** leaves

Dressing

2 tablespoons **olive oil**

1 teaspoon **sugar**

juice and grated zest of a **lime**

salt and **pepper**

1. Boil some water in a saucepan. Once boiling, add the tagliatelle. Cook for approximately 4 minutes or until tender. Drain and return to the pan. Add a few drops of olive oil and stir well. The olive oil prevents the tagliatelle from sticking together.

2. Mix the dressing ingredients together.

3. Put a little oil in a frying pan and fry the spring onions and the chilli for about 30 seconds.

4. Add the tuna, olives and the thyme to the pan and cook for 1 minute only, stir occasionally.

5. Tip the contents of the frying pan into the tagliatelle pan and carefully mix together.

6. Serve on the plates or bowls and drizzle the dressing over.

NOTE: The tuna, thyme and lime combination is great. A very tasty, fresh dish.

TIP: To deseed a chilli without cutting it in half, simply cut the green end off and roll between your hands and the seeds should all fall out. Always wash your hands with soap after chopping chillies and be careful not to touch or rub your eyes.

TIP: Take care not to overcook fresh tuna, it can easily become dry.

Tuna Steaks
with mini roasts, mangetout and anchovy sauce

4 medium **potatoes**

2 **tuna steaks**

200g pack of **mangetout** and **baby sweetcorn**

Sauce

5 **anchovy fillets**

1 tablespoon **olive oil**

juice of a **lemon**

1 **garlic** clove, chopped finely

½ teaspoon **sugar**

1 dessertspoon chopped **fresh basil**

1. Preheat the oven to 200°C fan oven/220°C/Gas 7. Put the mini roasts in the oven (see page 21).

2. Mix the sauce ingredients together in a bowl and stir well.

3. Put a pan of water on to boil for the mangetout.

4. About 5 minutes from the end of the cooking time for the potatoes, begin to cook the tuna. Heat a little oil in a frying pan, add the tuna and cook for about 1 minute each side. Overcooked tuna can be very dry. If you look at the side of the tuna you can see that it will have gone 'white' almost all the way through. Set aside but leave in the pan.

5. Add the mangetout and baby sweetcorn to the boiling water and cook for 1 minute.

6. Serve the tuna with the dressing, potatoes and mangetout.

NOTE: A sophisticated, simple, fresh recipe. Full of healthy stuff and tasty too.

TIP: Tuna can be eaten when it is a little pink in the middle and is better that way, rather than overcooked and dry.

WHERE ON EARTH: Anchovy fillets are sold in small jars or tins and are usually with the tinned fish over the freezers.

Mediterranean Cod
with sun-dried tomatoes and roast potatoes

6 **olives**, chopped

2 pieces of **sun-dried tomatoes**, chopped

juice of ½ **lemon**

1 clove **garlic**, finely chopped

¼ **red pepper**, finely chopped

oil for potatoes

3 large **potatoes**, cut into 1" cubes

2 **cod** or **haddock** steaks

sprig of **fresh rosemary**

salad to serve

---

1. Preheat the oven to 180°C fan oven/200°C/Gas 6.

2. In a bowl, mix together the olives, sun-dried tomatoes, lemon juice, garlic and peppers.

3. Put the potatoes on a baking tray, drizzle with oil and season with salt. Using your hands, make sure the oil is evenly distributed. Place in the oven.

4. Prepare a piece of foil large enough to wrap both pieces of fish. It is best if you double the foil. Place on a baking tray or flat casserole dish.

5. Put the fish on the foil and pile the tomato mixture equally on each piece of fish. Add the sprig of rosemary. Fold up the foil over the fish and seal. Place in the oven for 20 - 25 minutes, depending on the thickness of the steaks.

6. Check that the potatoes are not getting too browned and if they are, simply give them a quick turn on the tray.

7. Everything should be finished at about the same time. Take the fish out of the parcels and put onto the plates and spoon the juices over the fish. Serve with the mini roasts. You could also serve with salad or green veggies, e.g. broccoli or green beans.

NOTE: Easy to make. Just put in the oven alongside the potatoes. Wrapping the fish in foil keeps in all the flavour.

WHERE ON EARTH:
Sun-dried tomatoes are near the tomatoes, or in the 'speciality foods' section.

Friends Around

If you have friends around and you want to move on from the usual 'take-away' and treat them to something a bit more special, here are some great ideas for cooking for planned invasions and a few for the unplanned. The recipes are easily scaled up to cook for larger numbers. If you have friends around for the weekend, there are a few ideas to make breakfast more special.

Spanish Chicken
with shallots and red wine

8 **chicken thighs**

6 large **potatoes**

oil for coating

2 tablespoons **brown sugar**

1 tablespoon chopped fresh **flat leaf parsley**

green vegetables

crusty bread (optional)

Marinade

12 **shallots**, left whole

1 mug good **red wine**

2 cloves **garlic**, finely chopped

12 **black olives**, chopped

12 dried, ready-to-eat **apricots**, cut into slices

salt and **pepper**

1 teaspoon **dried oregano**

---

1. Put the chicken thighs in a large bowl together with the marinade ingredients. If possible leave to marinade overnight. 2 hours will be OK, but overnight is best.

2. Once the chicken has marinated, preheat the oven to 180°C fan oven/200°C/Gas 6.

3. Make the roast potatoes (see page 20).

4. Heat a little oil in a large frying pan. Take the chicken thighs out of the marinade and fry for 3 - 4 minutes each side or until the skin is browned. You can do this in batches if you don't have a large pan.

5. Add the marinade to the pan with all the chicken and bring to the boil. Add the sugar. Cook for a few minutes.

6. Transfer to an ovenproof dish and cover, using foil if you do not have a dish with a lid. Cook in the oven for 30 - 35 minutes. The sauce should thicken whilst in the oven.

7. Stir in the parsley at the end of the cooking time.

8. About 15 minutes from the end of the cooking time, put the green beans on to cook. Everything should come out of the oven at the same time.

9. Serve with vegetables or crusty bread.

NOTE: In the past, we have cooked this for 30 people at one of Tim's birthday parties. We did need to borrow a few large pans, but, other than that, it is fairly easy to scale up. The sauce from this dish is yummy and the recipe makes quite a lot. Crusty bread is a must for mopping up the excess, either that or you'll be wanting to lick the plate clean!

Beef Bourguignon
with cheddar and mustard mash

1 tablespoon **olive oil**

10 - 12 **shallots** (small round onions)

2 rashers **bacon**, chopped finely

1 kg **stewing beef**, cubed

1 tablespoon **flour**

2 teaspoons concentrated **liquid**

beef stock, or 1 **stock cube** + 1 mug **water**

1 mug **red wine**

12 **mushrooms**, halved

2 sprigs **fresh rosemary**

2 **bay leaves**

6 - 8 medium **carrots**

1" cube **butter**

Mash

6 large **potatoes**

2" cube **butter**

1 mug grated **cheese**

1 tablespoon **wholegrain mustard**

1. Preheat the oven to 180°C fan oven/200°C/Gas 6.

2. Heat the oil in a 'hob to oven casserole' or large saucepan. Add the shallots and bacon and fry for 2- 3 minutes. Add the beef and fry until no longer pink and beginning to brown.

3. Add the flour and stir to distribute evenly. Allow to cook for 1 minute, stirring all the time.

4. Add the stock, water and wine. Bring to the boil, stirring. The liquid should thicken.

5. Add the mushrooms, rosemary and bay leaves to the pan.

6. If using a saucepan, transfer the contents of the pan to a casserole dish. Place the lid on and cook in the oven for 1½ hours. Stir occasionally.

7. When the casserole has been in the oven 45 minutes, peel the carrots and cut into large chunks. Place in a small ovenproof dish. Add the 1" cube of butter, ¼ mug water and plenty of salt and pepper. Cover with a lid or foil and put in the oven for the rest of the cooking time.

8. Make the mustard mash (see page 19). Serve.

NOTE: Beef Bourguignon was originally a French peasant recipe, which has been refined, until it has become a standard of French cuisine. It needs to be cooked slowly, but will wow the guests when you cook it.

WHERE ON EARTH:
Shallots are small, round onions found in the onion section of the veggies. They are not spring onions, which are sometimes referred to as shallots in Oriental cooking.

Sichuan Chicken
with tahini and peanut sauce

4 **chicken breasts**

1 **cucumber**, sliced into long thin strips

8 **spring onions**, sliced into long thin strips

Pancakes

2 **eggs**

2 mugs plain **flour**

1 mug **milk** + 1 mug **water**

Trex or **white Flora** to fry (you can use oil but a lard type is best)

Sauce

1 teaspoon freshly ground **black pepper**

4 tablespoons **soy sauce**

4 tablespoons **sugar**

4 tablespoons **white wine vinegar**

4 tablespoons **tahini paste**

4 tablespoons smooth **peanut butter**

¼ mug of **water**

---

1. Make the pancakes. Put the ingredients (apart from the white Flora) in a bowl and mix thoroughly with a whisk or spoon.

2. Heat a small amount of lard in a frying pan. When the fat is hot, pour approximately 2 tablespoons of the mixture into the pan, tipping the pan around so that the mixture spreads as thinly as possible over the surface of the pan. Let the mixture cook for about 1 minute. Gently lift the edge of the pancake to see if it is browned. Once browned, turn the pancake with a fish slice, then cook the other side.

3. Set aside until needed. If you have a particularly big frying pan, you may wish to cut the pancakes in half.

4. Make the sauce by mixing all the ingredients together in a bowl.

5. Pan roast the chicken (see page 16). Remove from the pan and cut into very thin slices.

6. Serve pancakes, sauce, chicken, cucumber and onions separately and allow people to make up their own pancakes.

NOTE: Full of flavour and a less expensive, different take on Peking Duck.

TIPS: If time is short, you can buy Peking Duck pancakes from the supermarket.

WHERE ON EARTH: Tahini paste is found with the 'speciality' foods.

Easy Cooked Breakfast
with hash browns

Hash browns

2 medium **potatoes**, grated

1 small **onion**, grated

1 **egg**

salt and **pepper**

8 **sausages**

8 slices of streaky **bacon**

2 large **tomatoes**, each cut in ½ horizontally

4 **eggs**

crusty bread or **toast**

oil

fruit juices

tea or **coffee**

1. Preheat the oven to 200°C fan oven/220°C/Gas 7.

2. Make the hash browns. In a large mixing bowl, combine the potato and onions, squeeze out the excess liquid with your hands and discard the liquid. Mix in the egg and season well with salt and pepper. Form into 4 small cakes.

3. Grease 4 baking trays with oil.

4. Place the hash browns on two of the trays, the sausages on another and the bacon on the final tray.

5. Put the sausages in the oven.

6. After 10 minutes put the hash browns in the oven.

7. After another 5 minutes put the bacon in the oven.

8. After another 10 minutes, make spaces between the sausages and bacon and add the tomatoes to the trays. Cook for a further 10 minutes.

9. While the tomatoes are cooking, fry 4 eggs.

10. Plate it all up and serve with lots of crusty bread or toast.

NOTE: A cooked breakfast for a large number of people is often difficult to produce in terms of getting the timing right, with all the pans on the hob spitting their fat at you! Here is an ordered and simple method to decrease the stress, where most of the food actually goes in the oven. So for a fry up without too much frying, read on...

Fresh and Fancy Saturday Breakfast
with smoothies, pain au chocloat and cinnamon toast

CINNAMON TOAST

6 slices of **bread**

2 tablespoons **sugar**

1 teaspoon **cinnamon**

butter

1. Toast one side of the bread under a grill.

2. Butter the untoasted side.

3. Mix the sugar and cinnamon in a bowl and sprinkle over the buttered side.

4. Grill until they brown or the sugar starts to bubble.

5. Cut into triangles and serve.

PAIN AU CHOCOLAT

1 x 375g pack of ready-rolled **puff pastry**

100g bar of **milk chocolate**

1 **egg**, beaten

1. Preheat the oven to 200°C fan oven/220°C/Gas 7. Grease a large baking tray with butter or spread.

2. On a floured surface, unroll the pastry with the longest side toward you, cut in half horizontally and in three vertically, giving you 6 squares.

3. Roughly chop approximately half the chocolate. Share evenly between the squares of pastry, leaving small gaps round the edges of each piece.

4. Wet the edges of the squares with a little water, using your fingers. This helps the pastry to stick together.

5. Fold over each piece of pastry to make oblong pockets with the chocolate inside. Press down the three edges, not the folded edge.

6. Brush with the beaten egg (spread the egg with your fingers if you don't have a brush).

7. Grate the remaining chocolate over the top of each pain au chocolat.

8. Place in the oven for 12 - 15 minutes until they are golden brown.

TIP: Keep the ingredients for the pain au chocolat in your store. The pastry only requires one hour to defrost, or overnight in the fridge.

STRAWBERRY AND BANANA SMOOTHIE

1 **banana** broken up a little

½ x 500g punnet of **strawberries**

1 dessertspoon **honey**

1 mug **apple juice**

BLUEBERRY AND GREEK YOGURT SMOOTHIE

300 ml of **Greek yogurt**

200g punnet **blueberries**

1 dessertspoon **honey**

1 mug **apple juice**

NOTE: Healthy, simple way to feed breakfast to a good number of people. The pain au chocolat are easy to make and delicious when fresh.

1. For each smoothie, all you need to do is blitz the ingredients, adding enough apple juice to give your desired consistency.

2. Enjoy!

Beef Enchilada
with sweetcorn and avocado salsa

£3.00 /PERSON

EASE ★★★★

SERVES 4

PREP 35 MINS

COOK 15 MINS

Enchilada Filling

1 **onion**, chopped

2 cloves **garlic**, chopped finely

500g **beef mince**

1 x 400g tin **chopped tomatoes**

1 teaspoon **sugar**

2 fat **red chillies**, cut into thin slices

2 teaspoons **cumin**

2 teaspoons liquid **beef stock**, or 1 beef stock cube

1 tablespoon **tomato purée**

salt and **pepper**

Tomato Sauce

1 x 400g **tin tomatoes**

1 tablespoon **tomato purée**

1 teaspoon **sugar**

8 **corn tortillas**

---

1. Preheat oven to 220°C fan oven/240°C/Gas 9.

2. Heat a little oil in a saucepan. Fry the onions and garlic for 2 minutes until they become soft.

3. Add the mince and fry until it is no longer pink.

4. Add the chopped tomatoes, sugar, chilli, cumin, beef stock and tomato purée. Cook for about 5 minutes, the mixture should be quite thick, not runny. Season with salt and pepper. Leave to cool slightly.

5. Mix the tomato sauce ingredients and whizz with a hand-held blender.

6. Mix the white sauce ingredients in a bowl.

7. Grease a large ovenproof dish with oil. Divide the meat mixture between the 8 tortillas and roll each one up. Place side by side in the dish.

8. Pour over the tomato sauce and then pour the white sauce on top of that.

9. Place in the oven for 10 - 15 minutes or until the top begins to brown.

10. While the enchiladas are cooking, prepare the salsa by mixing all the ingredients in a bowl.

NOTE: A little more fiddly to make, but not difficult. The sour cream sauce is delicious and contrasts well with the spiciness of the rest of the dish.

WHERE ON EARTH: Corn tortillas are with the other Mexican foods, often near the tinned tomatoes.

Simple white sauce

300ml carton of **soured cream** or **crème fraîche**

1 tablespoon chopped **basil**

1 mug grated cheddar **cheese**

Sweetcorn and avocado salsa

2 tablespoons **olive oil**

1 **avocado**, peeled and cut into chunks

juice of 1 **lemon**

3 **spring onions**, chopped

1 teaspoon **sugar**

2 **tomatoes**, chopped into chunks

½ x 340g tin **sweetcorn**

Cajun Chicken Salad
with bacon and potatoes

2 large **potatoes**

oil

5 rashers of **streaky bacon**

2 tablespoons **Cajun seasoning**

2 **chicken breasts**

4 **spring onions**, sliced

1 x 100g bag **green salad**

1 **avocado**, peeled and cut into chunks

salt and **pepper**

Dressing

1 tablespoon **olive oil**

juice of a **lime**

1 teaspoon **sugar**

salt and **pepper**

---

1. Preheat the oven to 200°C fan oven/220°C/Gas 7.

2. Peel the potatoes and cut into 1" dice. Place on a baking tray and pour over oil. Season with salt, distribute the oil evenly using your hands. Place in the oven for 25 - 30 minutes or until the potatoes are brown.

3. While the potatoes are cooking, combine the dressing ingredients in a bowl and set aside.

4. Heat a little oil in a frying pan and fry the bacon until it is crispy. Once cooled, cut into pieces and set aside.

5. Pour the Cajun seasoning into a shallow dish. Place the chicken breasts in the dish and coat evenly with the seasoning.

6. Pan roast the chicken breast (see page 16).

7. Leave the chicken breast to cool a little before cutting into thin strips.

8. Mix the salad in a large bowl with bacon, avocado and the spring onions.

9. When the potatoes are cooked, drain any excess oil and mix with the salad.

10. Arrange the salad on individual plates. Arrange the chicken on top of the salad. Drizzle the dressing over the top of each plate.

NOTE: This is a different take on the usual Cajun chicken with chips or wedges. The avocado makes a yummy contrast to the spice on the chicken.

Sasuage Rolls
with potato wedges and tomato sauce

4 large **potatoes**, cut into wedges

oil

1 x 375g packet **ready rolled puff pastry**, defrosted

8 fat **sausages** with skins taken off

Tomato and Basil Sauce

1 **onion**, sliced

1 x 400g **tin tomatoes**

2 tablespoon **fresh basil**, chopped

1 teaspoon freshly ground **black pepper**

1 tablespoon **tomato purée**

1 tablespoon **white wine vinegar**

1 teaspoon **sugar**

oil to fry

1. Preheat the oven to 180°C fan oven/200°C/Gas 6.

2. Make the potato wedges and put in the oven (see page 21).

3. Spread out the pastry, cut in half lengthways. Put 4 sausages, end to end, down the centre of each strip of pastry. Wet one edge of each strip with a little water, using your fingers. This will make the 2 layers of pastry stick together.

4. Fold the pastry over and pinch together the edge. Cut each strip into 8 pieces.

5. Place on a lightly greased baking tray and place in the oven for 15 - 20 minutes. The rolls should be golden brown.

6. While the sausage rolls are in the oven, make the tomato sauce. Heat the oil in a saucepan and fry the onions until they begin to brown.

7. Add the rest of the ingredients and bring to the boil. Simmer gently for 5 - 6 minutes. Take off the heat and blitz with a hand-held blender.

8. Serve the rolls and sauce together with the wedges.

NOTE: With ready rolled pastry, sausage rolls are simple to make and much better than anything you will buy in the supermarket. You can buy different flavoured, good quality sausages. Well worth the effort.

TIP: To get the skins off the sausages, simply make a slit down the side of each sausage and peel the skin off.

£1.55 /PERSON	EASE ★★	SERVES 3-4	PREP 25 MINS

Fruity Chicken Salad
with croutons

1 small ready-cooked chicken or 2 pan-fried **chicken breasts** (see page 16)

1 **little gem lettuce**, cut horizontally into strips

1 green **apple**, cored and thinly sliced

1 **orange**, with peel cut off and segments cut out

3 **spring onions**, chopped

2 sticks **celery,** finely sliced

⅓ **cucumber,** cut into long sticks

½ mug **pecan nuts**, very roughly cut

1 slice of **bread** to fry

olive oil to fry

Dressing

1 teaspoon **Korma curry paste**

2 tablespoons **natural yogurt**

2 tablespoons **mayo**

1 teaspoon **sugar**

juice of 1 **lemon**

1. Pull apart the chicken or cut up the chicken breasts into strips.

2. Heat a little oil in a frying pan and cook the curry paste for 30 seconds. Leave to cool.

3. Mix the rest of the salad ingredients together in a bowl and add the chicken.

4. Mix together the dressing ingredients.

5. Make the croutons (see page 17).

6. Mix the dressing into the salad and serve with the croutons.

NOTE: Very appealing, sweet and savoury salad, with the extra crunch coming from the croutons.

TIP: This is so easy to make if you have friends call in unexpectedly. Buy a cooked chicken from the supermarket along with the salad ingredients. Try to keep the dressing ingredients in your store cupboard.

Quick and Crunchy Chicken Salad
with mayo and mustard dressing

1 small **ready-cooked chicken**

2 thick slices of **ham**, cut into strips

10 - 12 very thin slices of **cheddar cheese**

2 sticks of **celery**, chopped

4 **spring onion**s, cut lengthways to make thin strips

1 **green apple**, cored and cut into thin wedges

2½" **cucumber,** cut into sticks

2 **little gem lettuce**, cut thinly across the lettuce to form strips

Crusty bread to serve.

Dressing

4 tablespoons **mayo**

3 tablespoons **olive oil**

juice of a **lemon**

2 teaspoons **wholegrain mustard**

2 teaspoons **sugar**

salt and **pepper**

1. Dismantle the chicken and gently pull apart into long strips. Mix with the rest of the salad ingredients.

2. Mix the dressing ingredients together.

3. Divide onto the appropriate number of plates and drizzle over the dressing.

4. Serve with the crusty bread.

NOTE: This is a great idea if friends call to say they are on their way. Pop to the supermarket and buy these simple ingredients. If you have a crowd coming, just multiply the ingredients. The salad looks really good if you cut everything into long thin strips.

BBQ

Make your BBQs something more than the standard cheap burgers and plastic cheese squares. This gives a good guide in planning a BBQ. Get friends to pitch in on the preparation and make sure the person cooking at the barbeque can cook!

A trick to avoiding disasters is to never cook things over a flame, as they will burn on the outside before they are cooked through. Wait until the flames have died down and you just have hot coals. Be patient. Don't be tempted to put things on to cook before this point. Another tip is to use a BBQ with a lid. It will act like an oven and keep heat around the food you are cooking. This will help with cooking meat all the way through.

Once you know the approximate number of people coming to the BBQ, choose from the selection below. Depending on appetites, allow 4 - 5 meat/fish portions per person and 3 - 4 salad portions per person.

Chicken Kebabs
makes 12 - 15

4 **chicken breasts**, each breast cut into 6

4 **red onions**, each cut into 6 wedges

6 **tomatoes**, cut in 4s

12 **mushrooms**, cut in half

3 **red peppers**, cut into 12 pieces each

wooden skewers

Marinade

2 tablespoons **soy**

1 tablespoon **sugar**

2 tablespoons **oil**

1 tablespoon **honey**

1 tablespoon chopped fresh **basil**

salt and **pepper**

1. Mix the marinade ingredients in a large bowl and add the chicken. Leave for 1 hour.

2. Soak the wooden skewers in water, this should stop them burning too much when you BBQ them.

3. Distribute all the ingredients across the skewers (around 9 pieces per skewer).

4. When you BBQ, make sure the chicken is cooked all the way through by testing a large piece.

Potato Wedges
enough for 12 to have the equivalent of 1 potato

12 large **potatoes**, cut into wedges   **oil**

1. Preheat the oven to 200°C fan oven/220°C/Gas 7.

2. Place the potatoes on a baking tray, drizzle with oil and season with salt and pepper. Place in the oven, when the BBQ is just about ready to cook on. Cook for 25 minutes. It may be better to cook 2 trays at a time. In this way, you have a supply of freshly cooked wedges throughout the BBQ.

Burgers
makes approximately 16 medium sized burgers

1. Mix everything together really well with your hands to make as smooth as possible.

2. Form into burgers. Don't make them too big, as this will make it easier to ensure that they are cooked right through.

1 kg **beef mince**

1 **egg**, beaten

1 **onion**, finely chopped

6 pieces of **sun-dried tomatoes**, chopped finely

salt and **pepper**

Chicken Pieces
makes 18 pieces/portions

1. Cut the chicken breasts lengthways into 3 pieces. This makes it easier to ensure that the meat is cooked through.

2. Mix together the rest of the ingredients to form a marinade. Add the chicken, cover with cling film and leave for 2 hours in the fridge.

6 **chicken breasts**

2 tablespoons **soy sauce**

2 teaspoons grated **fresh ginger**

2 tablespoons **oil**

1 tablespoon **honey**

BBQ Trout

1 trout, wrapped in foil, will take about 10 minutes to cook in the barbeque with the lid down.

If you are having a large crowd, you can buy a whole salmon. Cook it in the same way as the trout, but it will take much longer to cook, say, 25 - 35 minutes, depending on size. Just keep testing to see if it is cooked.

Salads to serve with the BBQ

Green Salad, enough for 12 portions

2 **lettuce**, washed and cut into bite-sized pieces

2 bunches **spring onions**, chopped

1 **cucumber**, chopped

1 **fennel bulb**, sliced

Simple dressing

3 tablespoons **oil**

3 tablespoons **wine vinegar**

3 teaspoons **sugar**

salt and **pepper**

1. Just before serving, mix the green salad ingredients together and sprinkle over the dressing.

2. Grate some Parmesan over the top.

Potato Salad, enough for 12 portions

1 kg bag of **new potatoes**

¼ x 500g pack of **frozen peas**

3 **spring onions**, chopped

2 tablespoons **crème fraîche**

1 tablespoon **mayo**

2 tablespoons chopped **fresh mint**

1. Cut the potatoes into 1" pieces and boil for 10 - 15 minutes until tender. Add the peas 5 minutes before the end of the cooking time. Drain the water and return to the pan.

2. Once the potatoes and peas are cooked and cooled, mix all the ingredients together.

Rice Salad makes enough for 12 to have a portion.

1 mug **rice**, cooked in 2 mugs water with 1 teaspoon **pilau rice seasoning**

1 x 340g can **sweetcorn** (drained)

2 green **eating apples**, cored and cut into small chunks

handful of **sultanas** or **raisins**

6 **spring onions**, chopped

2 tablespoons chopped fresh **basil** or **chives**

3 tablespoons **mayo**

2 tablespoons **olive oil**

juice of a **lemon**.

1. Cook the rice in the water with the Pilau rice seasoning (see page 22 for more details).

2. Once the rice is cooked and cooled, mix with the other ingredients.

Vegetable Kebabs
makes 15

1. Mix the marinade ingredients in a large bowl and add the vegetables. Leave for 1 hour.

2. Soak the wooden skewers in water, as this should stop them burning too much when you BBQ them.

3. Arrange evenly on the kebab skewers (approximately 8 pieces per skewer).

4 red **onions**, cut into 6 wedges each

6 **tomatoes**, cut into 4s

12 **mushrooms**, cut in half

3 **red peppers**, cut into 12 pieces each

3 **courgettes,** cut into thick slices

wooden skewers

Marinade

2 tablespoons **soy**

2 tablespoons **oil**

1 tablespoon **sugar**

1 tablespoon **honey**

salt and **pepper**.

BBQ Bananas

Cut open a banana, lengthways, but do not pull the skin off. Push some pieces of chocolate into the banana and wrap them in foil. Cook on the BBQ, it will take 10 - 15 minutes, depending how hot it is. The banana should soften inside the skin and the chocolate will have melted. Serve in the skins with some ice cream.

BBQ Tips

Choose from the above recipes, you do not need to attempt everything each time you BBQ. Make sure everything is prepared before you begin to cook on the BBQ. It is best not to attempt a BBQ without a few helpers. Half the fun is preparing together and everyone wants a go at the cooking.

Sausages usually contain a lot of fat, which drips down onto the BBQ and will cause flames and burnt food. The idea is not to have flames licking the food.

If you cook all the same type of food at one time, it is easier to assess the right cooking times. This way, food will be neither undercooked nor overcooked.

Tapas

Tapas originates in Spain and has become quite trendy. It basically consists of lots of small dishes, which are shared together. There are many dishes you can chose from. Here are just a few. Choose 3 or 4, depending on how many people you have around.

You will need bread to go with some of these dishes, so buy some French sticks or cheese focaccia.

Tuna Empanadas

450g packet of **shortcrust pastry**

1 tablespoon **olive oil**

1 small **onion**, chopped

1 dessertspoon **tomato purée**

2 large **tomatoes**, chopped

½ **red pepper**, chopped

1 tablespoon **fresh basil**, chopped

185g tin **tuna**, drained of oil

salt and **pepper**

1. Make the filling. Heat a little oil in a frying pan and add the onions and peppers. Fry until the onions begin to brown. Add the tomatoes and tomato purée and cook for 2 minutes. Add the tuna and basil and stir. Take off the heat. Season well.

2. Preheat the oven to 180°C fan oven/200°C/Gas 6. Lightly grease a couple of baking trays.

3. Unroll the pastry. Cut approximately 6 squares. Put about 1 tablespoon of the filling in each one, then wet the edges with a little water and pinch them together to make a small patty.

4. Place on the trays and cook in the oven for 25 - 30 minutes.

Red Onion and Orange Salad

1 **red onion**, thinly sliced

4 **oranges**

1 tablespoon **fresh mint**, chopped

2 tablespoons **olive oil**

1 tablespoon **wine vinegar**

1 teaspoon **sugar**

12 - 15 **olives**, roughly chopped

salt and **pepper**

1. Cut the peel off the oranges and cut them into slices. Arrange them on a plate.

2. Mix together the oil, vinegar, sugar, chopped mint, olives and salt and pepper. Add the onions and mix. Place them over the oranges. Keep in the fridge until you need them.

Olives

2 tablespoons **olive oil**

½ **fat red chilli**, finely chopped

1 clove **garlic**, finely chopped

1 tablespoon freshly chopped **herbs**

salt and **pepper**.

1. Simply mix all the ingredients above and serve in small bowls.

Meatballs in Tomato Sauce

500g **minced beef**

1 **egg**, beaten

salt and **pepper**

Sauce

2 x 400g tins of **chopped tomatoes**

2 **onions**, chopped

2 cloves **garlic**, chopped finely

1 teaspoon **mixed herbs**

1 tablespoon **balsamic vinegar**

2 teaspoons **sugar**

2 tablespoons **tomato purée**

1 mug **water** + 1 **beef stock cube**, crumbled

salt and **pepper**

1. Make the sauce. Heat a little oil in a large saucepan and fry the onions and garlic, until the onions are soft. Add the rest of the sauce ingredients and bring to the boil. Season well.

2. Put the meat, egg, salt and pepper in a bowl and mix. Make small meatballs, should make about 30. Once you have made them all, add them to the tomato sauce and simmer for 15 minutes. Stir occasionally, but very gently, in order to keep the meatballs whole.

Chorizo in Cider

1. Heat a little oil in a pan and fry the onions and chorizo until they are browned.

2. Add the paprika and the cider and simmer gently for 10 - 15 minutes. Add the basil and serve with bread.

1 tablespoon **olive oil**

1 small **onion**, sliced

1 teaspoon **paprika**

1 mug **cider**

2 **chorizo sausages**, cut into slices

1 tablespoon **fresh basil**, chopped

Stuffed Mushrooms

8 large **flat mushrooms**, stalks removed

1 small **onion**, finely chopped

2 cloves **garlic**, finely chopped

½ **fat red chilli**, chopped

8 slices of **goats cheese**

3 tablespoons **olive oil**

1 tablespoon of **thyme leaves**, chopped

1. Preheat the oven to 180°C fan oven/200°C/Gas 6. Grease a large casserole dish.

2. Mix together in a bowl the olive oil, onion, garlic, chilli, thyme leaves and salt and pepper. Distribute, evenly, on top of the mushrooms and place in the casserole dish. Roast for 10 minutes.

3. Take them out of the oven and place a slice of the goats cheese on each one. Season with salt and pepper, drizzle with oil and return to the oven for 7 - 8 minutes.

Chickpea and Spinach Tapas

1. Heat a little oil in a wok, fry the peppers and the chickpeas for 2 - 3 minutes.

2. Add the spinach and cook for 30 seconds, or until it begins to wilt. Mix with the rest of the ingredients. Serve on toast, or crusty bread.

200g pack **fresh spinach**

400g tin **chickpeas**

1 **red pepper**, finely chopped

juice of 1 **lemon**

2 tablespoons **olive oil**

salt and **pepper**

Roasted Almonds

1. Preheat the oven to 200°C fan oven/220°C/Gas 7.

2. Spread the almonds on a baking tray and roast for 6 minutes.

3. Take them out of the oven and drizzle the oil over them. Add the salt and mix everything together.

2 x 220g packets of **blanched almonds**

1 dessertspoon **olive oil**

2 teaspoons **freshly ground sea salt**

Prawns and Hot Pepper Dipping Sauce

2 x 180g packs of frozen, **large prawns**, defrosted

1 tablespoon **olive oil**

Sauce

4 cloves **garlic**, peeled and left whole

1 **large tomato**, halved

2 **fat red chillies**, deseeded

½ x 100g pack **blanched almonds**

½ x 100g pack of **hazelnuts**

2 **red peppers**, cut into chunks

1 tablespoon **oil**

1 tablespoon **red wine vinegar**

1. Preheat the oven to 200°C fan oven/220°C/Gas 7.

2. Put the tomato, peppers, garlic and chilli on a baking tray and drizzle with olive oil. Season well with salt and pepper. Put in the oven for 15 minutes.

3. Add the almonds and hazelnuts to the tray. Put in the oven for another 4 minutes. Leave to cool.

4. Once cooled, place in a bowl and add the wine vinegar. Blitz with a hand-held blender, to form a thick sauce.

5. Just before serving, heat the oil in a frying pan and very quickly fry the prawns.

6. Serve with the dipping sauce.

Birthday Cakes
with candles and fancy bits

250g block softened **butter**

1 mug **sugar**

4 **eggs**

1½ mugs **self-raising flour**

2 teaspoons **vanilla extract**

4 tablespoons cold **water**

Butter cream icing

100g **butter** (⅖ of a 250g block)

1½ mugs **icing sugar**

1 tablespoon **milk** (if required)

1. Preheat the oven to 180°C fan oven/200°C/gas 6.

2. Put 18 bun cases in the baking tins ready. Proper cake tins are really handy here.

3. Beat the butter and sugar together until it turns pale cream and is quite fluffy. Add the eggs, one at a time and beat well. Add the flour, don't beat the mixture, but fold in the flour carefully (see page 15). Add 4 tablespoons of water.

4. Divide the mixture between the bun cases. They should be quite full in order to 'peak' well.

5. Place in the oven for 20 - 25 minutes. They should bounce back when pressed gently.

6. Leave to cool before decorating.

7. To make the butter cream, beat together the butter and icing sugar. If you want the icing to be softer, you can add some milk.

8. Spread icing over the cooled cakes and decorate with whatever else you fancy.

NOTE: Making birthday cakes for your friends, makes them feel so special. Lots of small cakes seem to be in vogue right now.

TIP: If you want to make chocolate cakes, remove 1 large tablespoon of the flour and replace with a tablespoon of cocoa and don't add the vanilla extract when making the cake mixture. For chocolate icing, replace 1½ tablespoons of the icing sugar with 1½ tablespoons cocoa.

WHERE ON EARTH: Vanilla extract, not essence, is found in the 'speciality' section. It is a little more expensive than the essence but will last for a while and is worth it for the flavour.

Dinner
Parties

Does the thought of cooking a three-course meal for 6 - 8 people fill you with dread? You may be planning your first dinner party. My idea in these recipes is to take the slog and panic out of the whole event. The suggestions include fairly simple recipes and a time-line which helps in the order of cooking things. If you are planning a party for more than six, don't try to be a hero, get one of the guests to come and help!

12:00	**12:30**	**13:15**	**13.45**	**14.05**	**14:15**	**14:30**
Make the meringues, bake and leave to cool. Don't put the cream and fruit on yet.	Prepare the starter, you can prepare all the starter ingredients, make the pancakes and leave in the fridge to put together later.	Prepare the chicken breasts, cover and leave in the fridge until needed.	Prepare the salsa, but don't put the dressing on.	Cut up the potatoes and cover well with the oil. Cover with foil or cling film and leave in the fridge until needed.	Put the meringues together and return to the fridge.	Set the table and take a long break.

Mediterranean Dinner Party

 £5.50 /PERSON EASE ★★★★★ SERVES 6

Pancakes
with smoked salmon

Tomato & Feta Chicken
with mini roasts and salsa

Mini Pavlovas
with fresh raspberries

9:30
Put the
starter
together and
put the oven
on to heat
up.

19:55
Serve
starter.

20.00
Put the
potatoes
in the oven
and sit down
to eat with
your guests.

20:20
Cook the
chicken
breasts.
While they
are cooking,
put the
dressing on
the salsa.

20:30
If the
potatoes are
cooked turn
down the
oven until
the chicken
breasts are
cooked.

20:35
Serve the
main course.

21:15
Serve the
dessert.

Pancakes
with smoked salmon

£1.85 /PERSON   EASE ★★   MAKES 6   PREP 20 MINS

1. To make the pancake mixture, beat the 2 eggs in a bowl, add the flour, beat together. Add enough of the water to make a very thick creamy consistency. The amount of water needed will depend on the size of the eggs you are using.

2. Heat about 1 teaspoon of Trex or white Flora in a frying pan. Once is it almost 'smoking', add dessertspoons of the mixture to the pan in order to make small pancakes. You should be able to cook 4 pancakes at one time. Cook on each side for approximately 2 minutes until browned. You will need enough pancakes to give each guest two.

3. Leave in the fridge until about half an hour before the guests arrive.

4. Place a little dollop of the cream cheese on each pancake. Tear the salmon into thin strips and divide between the pancakes.

5. Make some curly strips of cucumber using a vegetable peeler. If you are serving the main meal with bistro salad, take out some of the good looking bits to decorate the pancakes.

6. These can now go into the fridge until the guests arrive and you are ready to eat.

2 **eggs**

1 mug **flour**

½ mug **water**

Trex or **white Flora** to fry

1 x 150g packet of **cream cheese**

300g **smoked salmon**

½ **cucumber**

Tomato and Feta Chicken
with mini roasts and salsa

Salsa

250g pack **cherry tomatoes**, cut each into 4 pieces

6 **spring onions**, chopped

1 x 400g tin **sweetcorn**

2 tablespoons fresh chopped **basil**

Dressing for Salsa

2 tablespoons **olive oil**

juice of a **lemon**

2 teaspoons **sugar**

salt and **Pepper**

6 **chicken breasts**

1 x 200g pack of **feta cheese**

6 pieces of **sun-dried tomatoes**, chopped

oil to fry

a few **cocktail sticks**

6 - 8 large **potatoes**

---

1. Preheat the oven to 200°C fan oven/220°C/Gas 7.

2. Cut the potatoes into 1" cubes and place on a baking tray. Drizzle with olive oil and season with salt. Mix together with your hands to distribute the oil well. Place in the oven for 25 minutes or until browned.

3. Make the salsa by mixing all the salsa ingredients together. Make the dressing by mixing the dressing ingredients together. Don't put the dressing on until you are ready to serve.

4. Make a horizontal cut about three quarters of the way through the chicken breasts and stuff them with the cheese and tomato. Stretch the chicken over the stuffing and fix together with the cocktail sticks.

5. Heat a little oil in a frying pan. Fry the chicken for 2 minutes each side on a high heat. Turn the heat down and cook, with a lid on the pan, for a further 4 minutes each side. Check to make sure the chicken is no longer pink inside by making a cut into one of the chicken breasts. Carefully take the cocktail sticks out of the chicken.

6. Put the dressing on the salsa.

7. Serve the chicken breasts with the mini roasts and the salsa.

Mini Pavlovas
with fresh raspberries

Meringue

4 **egg whites**

1 mug **caster sugar**

fruit, blueberries, kiwi fruit, peaches, strawberries or **raspberries**

600ml **double cream**, whipped until it is stiff (see page 15).

1. Preheat the oven to 150°C fan oven/170°C/Gas 3.

2. Put a piece of greaseproof paper on a baking tray. A trick to stop the paper from sliding all over the place when you come to spread out your meringues is to put a few spots of oil between the paper and the tray.

3. Put the egg whites in a clean bowl, if there is any grease in the bowl it will not work.

4. Whisk with the mixer until the egg whites make soft peaks .

5. Add the sugar a little at a time and keep whisking. The meringue will become 'glossy'. Don't be in a hurry, this process may take 3 - 4 minutes.

6. Once all the sugar is added, put the meringue on the greaseproof paper, making individual pavlovas, about 2 tablespoons per person. Place in the oven for 45 minutes.

7. After 45 minutes, switch off the oven. Leave in the oven for a further 20 minutes as it cools down.

8. Once the meringues are completely cooled, spread the whipped cream over it and add the fruit to the top.

18:30
Make the caramel sauce.

18:45
Make the soup but don't add the prawns.

19:15
Make the curry, once complete, leave to one side and reheat when ready.

19:45
Start to boil water for the rice.

19:50
Add the rice to the boiling water and leave simmering with the lid on. Keep at a very low heat.

19:55
Reheat the soup and add the prawns.

Thai Dinner Party

£4.05 /PERSON

EASE ★★★★★

SERVES 6

Hot & Sour Soup

Chicken & Cashew Curry

Banana & Coconut Pancak

20:00
Switch off the heat under the rice and serve the soup.

20:25
Reheat the curry.

20:25
Check that the rice is cooked, if not, simmer slowly.

20:30
Serve the curry and rice.

21:15
Make the pancakes (they are fun things to make so get some of the guests to help!).

21:35
Reheat the caramel sauce and cut up the bananas.

21:40
Serve the warm pancakes with the bananas and the sauce.

Hot and Sour Soup

| £1.45 /PERSON | EASE ★ | MAKES 6 | PREP 15 MINS |

1. Finely chop 6 of the prawns. Heat a little oil in a saucepan and fry the chopped prawns for 1 minute, stirring constantly.

2. Add the water and the curry paste and simmer for 5 minutes.

3. Add the rest of the ingredients to the pan, apart from the whole prawns and simmer for 3 - 4 minutes.

4. Add the prawns just before serving and cook them for 2 minutes.

500g good sized **prawns**

1 tablespoon **oil**

4 mugs **water**

2 tablespoons **red Thai curry paste**

2 tablespoons **tamarind paste**

2 teaspoons **turmeric**

2 tablespoons **fish sauce**

juice of 2 **limes**

1 tablespoon **sugar**

NOTE: This soup has a really unique taste. It will be different to anything your guests will have tasted before.

Chicken and Cashew Curry

1 tablespoon **oil** to fry

1 large **red onion**, chopped

4 **chicken breast**, cut into bite-sized chunks

1 x 400g can **coconut milk**

2 tablespoons **red curry paste**

1 tablespoon **fish sauce**

juice of a lime

2 teaspoons **sugar**

1 small **tin pineapple**, cut into small chunks

1 tablespoon **fresh coriander,** chopped

100g packet **cashew nuts**, chopped

1½ mugs **basmati rice**

3 mugs **water**

1 **cucumber,** cut into sticks

1. Cook rice. See page 22.

2. Heat the oil in a large saucepan or wok. Fry the onions for 1 - 2 minutes until they become soft.

3. Add the chicken to the pan and cook until it is no longer pink.

4. Add the coconut milk, curry paste, fish sauce, lime juice, and sugar and cook for 4 - 5 minutes.

5. Add the pineapple, coriander, and cashew nuts and heat through.

6. Serve with the rice and cucumber sticks.

Banana and Coconut Pancakes
with caramel sauce

4 **eggs**

10 tablespoons **plain flour**

milk

8 tablespoons of **desiccated coconut**

Trex or white Flora to fry (you can use **oil**, but a lard type is best)

3 - 4 **bananas**

Caramel Sauce

150g **butter** (measure with the markings on the paper)

1 mug **sugar**

¼ mug **milk or cream**

---

1. Beat the eggs and flour together in a bowl or jug. Gradually add the milk, making sure there are no lumps. The mixture should be as thin as single cream, quite thin, but not as thin as milk. Stir in the coconut.

2. Heat about ½" cube of lard in a frying pan. When the fat begins to smoke a little, pour approximately 2 tablespoons of the mixture into the pan. Tip the pan around so that the mixture spreads over the surface of the pan. Let the mixture cook for about 1 minute.

3. Gently lift the edge of the pancake to see if it is browned. Once browned, turn the pancake with a slotted turner or toss and then cook the other side.

4. To make the caramel sauce, melt the butter over a low heat and add the sugar. Stir until the sugar is dissolved. Add the milk or cream a little at a time, being careful it does not 'spit' at you. Stir and heat for 1 minute. You should have a good, creamy sauce.

5. Chop up the bananas and spread them evenly across each pancake, cover with the sauce and serve.

Waiting for Pay Day

It's coming to the end of the month and you might have slightly overspent somewhere along the line! Having no money doesn't mean you have to revert to beans on toast. Here are a few ideas to try if you want something a bit more inspiring.

| £2.00 /PERSON | EASE ★ | SERVES 2-3 | PREP 40 MINS |

Crab Frittata
with green salad and lemon dressing

2 medium **potatoes**, cut into small cubes

oil to fry

1" cube of **butter**

6 **eggs**, beaten together with 1 tablespoon cold water and seasoned well

4 **spring onions**, chopped

170g can of **crab meat**, drained

1 tablespoon chopped **fresh basil**

½ mug grated **cheddar cheese**

salt and **pepper**

½ bag **green salad**

Dressing for salad

1 tablespoon **olive oil**

juice of ½ **lemon**

1 teaspoon **sugar**

salt and pepper

1. Heat the oven to 200°C fan oven/ 220°C/Gas 7.

2. Make mini roast potatoes (see page 21).

3. While the potatoes are cooking, prepare the rest of the ingredients for the frittata and mix together the salad dressing.

4. Once the potato cubes are nicely browned, take them out of the oven. Put the grill on to heat up.

5. Heat the frying pan and add the butter. Once the butter has melted add the beaten eggs. Allow them to cook on a high heat for 1 - 2 minutes until the egg at the bottom begins to set. Gently stir, so the rest of the egg has a chance to cook a bit.

6. Before the egg is cooked completely, take off the heat and add the potatoes, onions, crab and the basil, distributing them evenly around the pan. Sprinkle the cheese over the top.

7. Return the pan to a low heat and cook for 2 minutes.

8. Place the pan under a hot grill for 4 - 5 minutes until the cheese is browned and the egg is no longer wobbly or runny. If you have a saucepan with a plastic handle, be careful not to push the pan right under the grill.

9. Serve with green salad. Drizzle the dressing over the salad.

NOTE: If you are particularly hard up and waiting for pay day, you can replace the crabmeat with tuna.

Smoked Mackerel Fish Cakes
with salad and Marie Rose sauce

£1.15 /PERSON | EASE ★★★ | SERVES 2-3 | PREP 35 MINS

Fish Cakes

2 medium **potatoes**

1 tablespoon **crème fraîche** or **natural yogurt**

3 - 4 ready-to-eat **smoked mackerel**, approx. 250g pack

1 **egg**

2 slices of **bread**, made into breadcrumbs

Salad

Marie Rose Sauce

2 tablespoons **mayo**

1 teaspoon **tomato purée**

1 teaspoon **sugar**

1 teaspoon **wine vinegar**

1. Boil and mash the potatoes and allow to cool. Add the crème fraîche.

2. Mix the sauce ingredients together in a bowl.

3. Take the skin of the mackerel and flake into the potatoes. Season well with pepper and mix. Do not use salt, as the fish is salty enough. Form into 4 - 6 cakes.

4. Beat the egg and place in a bowl. Place the breadcrumbs in another bowl.

5. Dip each fish cake, first into the egg and then into the breadcrumbs, coating evenly. Set aside on a plate.

6. Heat a little oil in a frying pan. Fry the cakes for 2 minutes on each side until browned.

7. Serve with the salad and the sauce.

NOTE: Often fish cakes can be a little bland, but the strong flavour of smoked mackerel makes these fish cakes yummy.

TIP: Usually smoked mackerel is sold in vacuum packs. You can keep these in the fridge for a few weeks, until their sell by date. They are very handy.

TIP: To make breadcrumbs, it is best to use bread that is a little dry already and just blitz it with a hand blender.

Corned Beef Hash
with fried eggs

4 medium **potatoes**

1 **onion**, sliced

½ x 340g can of **corned beef**

2 **eggs**

oil to fry

salt and **pepper**

---

1. Cut the potatoes into 1" cubes and put in boiling, salted water. Boil for 10 - 12 minutes until they are tender. Drain and return to the pan.

2. Put a little oil in a frying pan and fry the onions until they begin to turn brown. Add the potatoes and fry until the potatoes begin to brown. You may need to add a little more oil.

3. Cut the corned beef into cubes and add to the frying pan. Cook until the beef begins to brown. Remove from the pan and keep warm.

4. Clean the frying pan and fry the 2 eggs.

5. Serve the eggs on top of the corned beef hash.

NOTE: Old fashioned? Possibly. Inexpensive? Certainly. Tasty? Definitely.

TIP: Allowing the hash time to brown, as it cooks in the frying pan, is key to its success.

Chinese Meatball Noodle Soup
with fresh ginger

Meatballs

250g **beef mince**

½ clove **garlic**, finely chopped

½ teaspoon **coriander**

¼ teaspoon **cumin**

1 dessertspoon **dark soy sauce**

1 small **egg**, beaten.

Sauce

1 small **onion**, finely sliced

1 clove **garlic**, finely chopped

1 teaspoon freshly grated **ginger**

2 **celery** sticks, cut into thin strips

2 small **sweet potatoes,** cut into small cubes

1 tablespoon **tomato purée**

2 mugs **water** + 1 tablespoon concentrated **liquid beef stock**

½ mug **frozen peas**

200g pack **fresh egg noodles,** or **ready-to-wok egg noodles**

oil to fry

1. To make the meatballs, mix together all the ingredients, apart from the egg.

2. Once mixed, add enough egg to make the mixture bind together. The mixture should not be sloppy.

3. Form into small balls. You should be able to make about 15 - 16.

4. Heat a little oil in a wok and fry the onions, garlic, ginger, celery and sweet potatoes for 2 - 3 minutes, stirring frequently.

5. Add the tomato purée, water, stock and peas and bring to the boil, then turn down to simmer for 5 minutes.

6. Carefully add the meatballs to the soup. Bring back to the boil, then turn down to simmer for 5 minutes.

7. Add the noodles and bring back to the boil. Once boiling, take off the heat. Serve.

NOTE: I learned this recipe from a Chinese friend. It's a great meal to cook for a crowd, but also tasty enough to make for one or two people. The Chinese would eat the bits in the bowl with chopsticks and then drink the soup that is left behind.

Pancetta Pasta
with mixed vegetables

4 - 5 'bunches' of **tagliatelle** or ½ x 500g pack

1 small **onion**, chopped

½ fat **red chilli**, deseeded and finely chopped

1 clove **garlic**, finely chopped

200g pack **pancetta** or **bacon lardons**

1 **courgette**, diced

1 **yellow pepper**, diced

150g pack **cherry tomatoes**, halved

oil to fry

Parmesan to grate on top (optional)

1. Put the tagliatelle into boiling water, bring to the boil and then turn down to simmer for 4 minutes. Drain, return to the pan and cover with a lid.

2. Heat the oil in a wok and add the onion, chilli and garlic, cook for 2 - 3 minutes.

3. Add the pancetta and cook for 3 - 4 minutes.

4. Add the courgette and peppers, cook for 2 minutes.

5. If the pancetta produces a lot of oil, spoon some of it off before the next step.

6. Add the tomatoes and cook for 1 - 2 minutes until the tomatoes soften. Season with salt and pepper.

7. Add the tagliatelle and mix together. Serve.

NOTE: A good, healthy and inexpensive, midweek meal.

TIP: You can buy packs of pancetta lardons and keep them in the fridge for a month or so. Makes good, quick standby meals.

Winter Warming Meat and Potato Pie
with a suet pastry crust

4 - 5 **potatoes**, sliced into 1 cm slices

1 large **onion**, chopped

750g pack of **beef mince**

1 tablespoon **flour**

1½ mugs **water**

1 tablespoon **concentrated beef stock** or 1 **stock cube**, crumbled

salt and **pepper**

a little **oil** to fry

salt and **pepper**

Pie topping

2 mugs self-raising **flour**

1 mug **suet**

½ mug grated, strong **Cheddar cheese**

1¼ mugs **water**

1 beaten **egg**

---

1. Preheat the oven to 180°C fan oven/200°C/Gas 6.

2. Boil the potatoes for 8 - 10 minutes. They do not need to be completely cooked as they will cook in the oven. Drain and set aside until needed.

3. Heat a little oil in a saucepan, add the onions and fry for 3 - 4 minutes until they soften.

4. Add the mince and cook until it is no longer pink. Add the flour and stir well.

5. Add the water and stock and bring to the boil. Season with salt and pepper. Turn down to simmer while you prepare the pie topping.

6. To make the pie topping, mix the dry ingredients together in a mixing bowl, then add enough water to make a soft dough.

7. Turn out onto a floured board and press or roll the dough out until it is big enough to cover the casserole dish.

8. Pour the meat mixture into a casserole dish. Arrange the potatoes over the meat.

9. Gently lift the topping from the surface and place over the potatoes. Trim off any excess.

10. Brush with the beaten egg and place in the oven for 25 - 30 minutes until the crust is golden brown.

NOTE: My mum would often make meat and potato pie when I was young. It is a good winter warmer and is ideal to eat one day and heat up in the microwave the next day. The suet pastry is so easy to make.

WHERE ON EARTH: Suet is found in the baking section of the supermarket. It is made from beef fat and is excellent for pastry.

Shiitake Mushroom Risotto
with Parmesan

⅕ x 250g block **butter**

1 **onion**, finely chopped

1 small clove **garlic**, finely chopped

⅔ mug **risotto rice**

2 mugs **water**

1 **vegetable stock cube**

120g pack of **shiitake mushrooms**, sliced

salt and **pepper**

1 tablespoon **fresh basil**, chopped

Parmesan cheese to serve

---

1. Melt the butter in a pan, add the onions and garlic and fry for 2 - 3 minutes until the onions are soft.

2. Add the rice and cook for 1 minute until the rice has absorbed the butter. Add the water and the stock cube. Bring to the boil, then turn down to simmer for 10 minutes. Stir every now and then.

3. Add the mushrooms and simmer for a further 5 - 6 minutes. Stir frequently. The rice should be cooked and most of the liquid absorbed. If not, then just add a little more water and cook for 2 - 3 more minutes.

4. Season well with salt and pepper and stir in the basil at the last minute.

5. Serve in a bowl with some freshly shaved Parmesan (use a vegetable peeler) over the top.

NOTE: The shiitake mushrooms give this dish a subtle but very pleasing flavour.

TIP: Risottos should not be dry, but creamy in texture. If you are a vegetarian, use Parmesan 'style' cheese for the topping.

French Onion Tart
with tomato and cucumber salsa

 V | £1.40 /PERSON | EASE ★★★★ | PORTIONS 8-10 | PREP 30 MINS | COOK 50 MINS

For the flan case

375g packet of ready rolled **shortcrust pastry**

or

⅕ x 500g pack **Trex** or **white Flora**

1½ mugs **self-raising flour**

6 tablespoons **water**

¼ teaspoon **salt**

For the filling

50g **butter** (see packet for measure)

2 tablespoons **olive oil**

3 large **onions**, peeled and sliced

4 large **eggs**

300ml carton of **double cream**

1 mug of grated **cheddar cheese**

Salsa

4 **tomatoes**, cut into small cubes

1 tablespoon **fresh basil**, chopped

3" (8 cm) piece of **cucumber**, halved, deseeded and finely sliced

2 tablespoons **olive oil**

2 tablespoons **white wine**

1. Preheat the oven to 180°C fan oven/200°C/Gas 6.

2. If you are using ready-rolled pastry, simply unroll the pastry and gently ease into a flan dish. Now go to step 5.

3. If you are making the pastry, put the Trex, flour and salt into a bowl and rub in the fat, gently passing the mixture through your fingers and thumbs until it resembles breadcrumbs.

4. Stir in the water and the mixture will make a soft ball. Handle as little as possible. Put onto a floured surface and roll out with a rolling pin. Lift from the surface and gently ease into a flan dish.

5. Heat the oil and butter in a frying pan. On a high heat, fry the onions until they are browned and soft. Browning them is essential to produce the flavour for this tart.

6. Beat the eggs in a bowl and add the cream and salt and pepper.

7. Arrange the onions in the pastry case and sprinkle the grated cheese over them. Pour over the egg mixture.

8. Bake in the oven for 45 - 50 minutes until the eggs and cream are set. Give the tart a little shake and check it does not wobble. The top of the tart should be nicely browned. If the tart still wobbles when shaken slightly, turn down the oven to 160°C fan oven/180°C/Gas 4 and cook for another 10 minutes.

9. While the tart is in the oven, make the salsa. Just mix everything together in a bowl.

10. Cut the tart into portions and serve with the salad and salsa.

Salsa cont...

vinegar or **cider vinegar**

1 teaspoon **sugar**

salt and **pepper**

salad to serve

NOTE: You will need an 8"
or 20 cm flan dish for this
recipe. The first time I ate
this was at a wedding in
Strasbourg. It is delicious.

Tuna Noodles
with honey and ginger dressing

Dressing

2 teaspoons **honey**

1 tablespoon **fish sauce**

1 tablespoon **white wine vinegar**

2 tablespoons **oil**

1 fat **red chilli**, deseeded and finely chopped

1 teaspoon grated **fresh ginger**

salt and **pepper**

3 **spring onions**, sliced lengthways

¼ **cucumber**, cut in half, seeds removed and sliced thinly

½ **red pepper,** sliced thinly

185g can **tuna**, drained

½ x 400g pack **fresh egg noodles**

---

1. Mix the dressing ingredients together in a bowl.

2. In another bowl, mix together the spring onions, cucumber, red pepper and the tuna.

3. Boil some water in the kettle, pour the water over the fresh egg noodles and leave to stand for 1 minute. Drain.

4. Divide the noodles between the plates, placing the tuna mix over the top. Drizzle over the dressing.

NOTE: The sweet and spicy dressing with this dish transforms the otherwise dull tuna into something special.

TIP: Wash your hands after handling the chilli and be careful not to rub your eyes.

TIP: You will find fish sauce with the 'world' foods, somewhere near the curry pastes etc.

£1.40 /PERSON EASE ★★★ SERVES 2-3 PREP 25 MINS

Pan Roasted Chicken
with spicy fried rice

1 mug **basmati rice** cooked in 2 mugs water

1 **chicken breast**

2 **eggs**, beaten

1 large **onion**, thinly sliced

1 clove **garlic**, finely chopped

½ **red pepper**, cut into fine dice

1 teaspoon freshly grated **ginger**

½ fat **red chilli**, you can add more if you like your food really hot

2 tablespoons **oyster sauce**

1 tablespoon **soy sauce**

2 tablespoons **water**

2 **spring onions**, cut into thin strips

---

1. Put the rice on to cook (see page 22).

2. Pan roast the chicken (see page 16). Once cooked, cut into thin slices.

3. Add a little oil to the pan, pour in the eggs and swish around the pan to form a very thin omelette. Cook for about 1 minute. Take out of the pan and leave to one side. Cut into thin strips.

4. Heat a little oil in the frying pan and add the onions, garlic, peppers and ginger. Cook until the onions are soft.

5. Add the chilli, oyster sauce, soy sauce and water and heat for 1 minute.

6. Stir in the cooked rice and heat through.

7. Add the sliced chicken and egg and mix together.

8. Serve garnished with the spring onions.

NOTE: This is a much fuller version of egg fried rice. Delightful.

WHERE ON EARTH: You can find oyster sauce with the other Oriental sauces and the curry pastes.

Lazy Days

Lazy days, are the odd Saturday or Sunday when life is a little more relaxed and maybe you have time to wait for things to cook more slowly. Cooking food slowly allows more time for flavours to develop and you end up with some amazingly, yummy food. Some of these recipes are great to cook at the weekend; that way you can have the 'leftovers' during the week.

Lamb Tagine
with couscous

1 tablespoon **oil**

2 large **onions**, chopped

1½ Kg **stewing lamb**

400g **tin tomatoes**

1 **vegetable stock cube** + 1 mug **water**

1 mug **ready-to-eat dried apricots**

½ x 100g pack **toasted almonds**

salt and **pepper**

1½ mugs **couscous**

3 mugs boiling **water**

4 **carrots**, peeled and chopped

2 **courgettes**, chopped

Spices

1 teaspoon **chilli powder**

1 teaspoon **ground coriander**

1 teaspoon **cumin**

1 teaspoon **ground ginger**

½ teaspoon **saffron** or 1 teaspoon **turmeric**

1 **cinnamon stick**

---

1. Preheat the oven to 180°C fan oven/200°C/Gas 6.

2. Heat the oil in a large saucepan, or 'hob to oven' casserole dish. Fry the onions until soft. Add the meat and cook until the meat is no longer pink and begins to brown.

3. Add all the spices and cook for 1 - 2 minutes.

4. Add the tomatoes, stock cube, water, apricots and almonds. Season well and bring to the boil.

5. Once boiling, transfer to a large casserole dish, put the lid on or cover with foil, and place in the oven to cook for 1½ - 2 hours. Stir a couple of times during the cooking. You may need to add a little more water if the tagine becomes dry.

6. 20 minutes before the cooking time is up for the tagine, put the carrots on to boil. After 10 minutes, add the courgettes in with the carrots.

7. Once the courgettes are on the boil, pour the hot water over the couscous in a bowl. Leave for 5 minutes.

8. Drain the vegetables and add to the cooked couscous and mix. Serve with the tagine.

NOTE: Tagines originate in Morrocco. You can buy Ras El Hanout, a special mix of 35 spices, used in tagines, in Morrocco. It is difficult to find it here, hence the longish list of spices.

TIP: Building up a stock of spices really helps. You can buy larger packets in Asian supermarkets and in some traditional supermarkets.

Pork Patties
with chilli dipping sauce

Dipping Sauce

2 teaspoons **cornflour**

½ mug **water**

1 fat **red chilli**, chopped

1 **spring onion**, finely chopped

2 tablespoons **wine vinegar**

2 tablespoons **tomato purée**

2 tablespoons **sugar**

1 mug **rice**

1 teaspoon **pilau rice seasoning**

1 **cucumber**, sliced diagonally

Patties

500g **pork mince**

2 **pork sausages**, skins removed

2 **spring onions**, finely chopped

1 **garlic** clove, chopped finely

zest of a **lemon**

1 teaspoon **ground coriander**

1 teaspoon **cumin**

2 tablespoons **oil** to fry

1. In a small saucepan, mix the cornflour with the water. Add the rest of the dipping sauce ingredients and bring to the boil, stirring frequently. Turn down the heat and simmer for 1 - 2 minutes. Leave to cool.

2. Make the pilau rice (see page 22).

3. Mix together the patty ingredients, use your hands to create a smooth paste. Form into small patties, make them quite flat and then they are easier to cook. The mixture should make about 12.

4. Heat the oil in frying pan. Once the oil is hot, add the patties. You may be able to cook 6 at a time. Cook on a medium/high heat for 2 - 3 minutes each side.

5. Serve with the rice, cucumbers and dipping sauce.

NOTE: These patties are a little fiddly, but delightful. The chilli sauce is much better than the bought variety.

TIP: Use a vegetable peeler to slice the cucumber. You will get really nice thin slices that way.

Puff Pastry Beef Parcels
with pine nuts and Parmesan

Tarts

1 **onion**, sliced

1 **garlic** clove, finely chopped

1 tablespoon **oil** + 1" cube **butter** to fry

1 teaspoon **sugar**

1 dessertspoon **fennel seeds**

1 x 375g pack of **ready-rolled puff pastry**

300g **beef mince**

125g **mozzarella cheese**, pulled apart

1 tablespoon **pine nuts**

¼ mug grated **Parmesan cheese**

Dressing

juice of one **lime**

1 dessertspoon **honey**

1 tablespoon **olive oil**

salt and **pepper**

bistro or **leaf** salad

---

1. Fry the onions and garlic in the oil and butter on a high heat until they are browned. Add the sugar and the fennel seeds and cook for 1 minute until the sugar is dissolved. Leave to cool.

2. Preheat the oven to 180°C fan oven/200°C/Gas 6.

3. Cut the pastry sheet into 4 squares. Place on a greased baking sheet.

4. Put the beef mince in a mixing bowl and season with salt and pepper. Work the mince together with your hands and make 4 patties.

5. Divide the onion mixture between the four pieces of pastry. Place a beef patty on top of each one.

6. Turn up the corners of the pastry and 'stick' them to the beef, using a dab of water on the corner of each square of pastry to do this.

7. Place in the oven for 15 minutes. Take out of the oven and add the mozzarella, pine nuts and Parmesan to the top of the patties. Return to the oven for another 10 minutes.

8. Mix together the salad dressing ingredients and prepare the salad.

9. Serve together while the tarts are hot.

NOTE: The fennel seeds in these tarts give them quite a unique flavour. The honey and lime dressing is also full of flavour.

Sunday Roast
with great roast potatoes

2 kg piece of **beef brisket**

sprig rosemary or 1 teaspoon **dried rosemary**

1 mug water + 1 tablespoon **liquid beef stock** or 1 **stock cube**

6 - 8 medium **potatoes**

1 **onion**, cut into wedges

6 - 8 **carrots**

1" cube **butter**.

green vegetables

Gravy

1 tablespoon **flour**

1 tablespoon softened **butter**

1. Preheat the oven to 180°C fan oven/200°C/Gas 6.

2. Put the meat in a casserole dish. Place the sprigs of rosemary under the strings holding the meat together. Add the water and stock and brush the top of the meat with oil. Season well and cover with a lid or foil. Place in the preheated oven for 1 hour.

3. After 1 hour, turn the oven down to 160°C fan oven/180°C/Gas 4 and cook for a further 2½ hours. During that time, the vegetables need to be cooked. See steps 4 - 6.

4. Cut the potatoes into quarters and place on a baking tray, together with the onion wedges. Drizzle with oil, season with salt and pepper and mix together with your hands. One hour before the end of the cooking time for the meat, turn up the oven to 180°C fan oven/200°C/Gas 6 and put the potatoes in.

5. Peel the carrots and cut into sticks (see picture). Place in an ovenproof dish with the butter and ¼ mug water. Cover with foil and place in the oven 30 minutes before the end of the cooking time for the meat.

6. Put water on to boil for the green vegetables. When the cooking time for the meat is finished, put the green vegetables on to boil. Simmer broccoli for 4 - 5 minutes, green beans for 8 - 10 minutes.

7. Take the meat out of the oven. If the potatoes and carrots are cooked, turn the oven down to keep them warm.

8. Take the meat out of the casserole dish and place on a board ready to carve. Leave to stand while you cook the gravy.

9. To make the gravy, pour the rest of the contents of the casserole dish into a saucepan. In a bowl, mix the butter and flour to a paste, add to the meat juices and stir well. Bring the gravy to the boil and simmer for 1 - 2 minutes. If the gravy is too thick, add a little water from the vegetables you have cooked.

10. Carve the meat and serve with the vegetables and the gravy.

1. 09:30
Put oven on to heat @ 180ºC fan oven/200ºC/Gas 6.

2. 09:45
Put meat in the oven.

3. 10:45
Turn oven down to 160ºC fan oven/180ºC/Gas 4.

4. 12:15
Turn the oven back up to 180ºC fan oven/200ºC/Gas 6 and put the potatoes in.

5. 12:45
Put carrots in the oven.

6. 13:15
Put greens on to cook.

7. 13:15
Take meat out of the oven.

8. 13:20
Drain the greens and leave in pan to stay warm.

9. 13:22
Make the gravy.

10. 13:30 ish
Carve the meat then serve.

Roast Chicken Dinner
with sweet potato mash, carrots and green beans

2 kg **chicken**

5 - 6 slices **streaky bacon**

1 **onion**, cut into wedges

1½ mugs **water**

1 teaspoon **liquid chicken stock** or 1 **stock cube**

6 - 8 **carrots**

1" cube **butter**

4 - 5 medium **potatoes**

Mash

4 sweet **potatoes**

2 x 1" cube **butter**

salt and **pepper**

Gravy

1 tablespoon **flour**

1" cube **butter**

1. Preheat the oven to 200°C fan oven/220°C/Gas 7.

2. Place the chicken in a large casserole dish. Rub some oil over the skin with your fingers. Put the bacon over the chicken. Place the onions in the dish along with the water and stock. Season well with salt and black pepper.

3. Cover, either with a lid or with foil, and put in the oven for 1 hour. After 1 hour, remove the lid or the foil to allow the chicken to brown and crisp.

4. While the chicken is cooking for the first hour, peel the carrots and cut into bite-sized pieces. Place in an ovenproof dish, add the butter and ¼ mug water. Season well and cover the dish with foil. Put in the oven for the 35 minutes before the end of the cooking time for the chicken.

5. Prepare the mash. Put half a pan of water on to boil. Peel the potatoes and sweet potatoes and cut into 2" chunks. Once the water is boiling, put the potatoes in. Bring to the boil, then turn down the heat and simmer for 10 - 15 minutes until the potatoes are tender. Drain and return to the pan, but retain the cooking liquid. Add the butter and the seasoning to the potatoes. Mash and leave in the pan with the lid on.

6. The chicken should be cooked by now. With a couple of forks or a fish slice, lift the chicken out of the casserole dish. Set to one side.

7. Put the green beans on to cook and simmer for 5 - 6 minutes. Drain and return to the pan to keep warm.

8. Carefully pour the contents of the casserole dish into a saucepan along with about 1 mug of the potato water. Skim off any fat with a spoon. Mix the flour and butter in a small bowl, add to the saucepan and whisk until smooth. Heat gently for a couple of minutes and you should have a lovely gravy.

9. Carve the chicken and serve with the gravy, mash, beans and carrots.

Moroccan Chicken
with green olives and lemon

1 tablespoon **oil**

1 **onion**, cut into wedges

2 cloves **garlic**, finely chopped

4 **chicken** thighs

½ **lemon**

½ x 200g pack of **blanched almonds**

¼ mug **raisins**

12 **green olives**, halved

1 mug **water** + 1 teaspoon **liquid chicken stock** or ½ stock cube

1 mug **rice**

1 tablespoon chopped **fresh coriander**

1. Put a little oil in a large saucepan or wok. Fry the onions and garlic until they become soft. Add the chicken thighs and fry until they become browned.

2. Cut the lemon into small chunks, including the zest and pith. Add to the pan.

3. Add the almonds, raisins, olives, water and stock to the pan, bring to the boil. Turn down the heat and simmer, with a lid on for 25 - 30 minutes until the chicken is tender.

4. Meanwhile, cook the rice (see page 22).

5. Add the coriander to the chicken just before serving.

NOTE: Here, chicken thighs are cooked in a delicious lemony sauce. The result is the most succulent chicken with a sweet and sour twist.

Beef Steak
with mash, balsamic onion and mustard sauce

Mustard sauce

2 tablespoons **crème fraîche** or **soured cream**

1 tablespoon **wholegrain mustard**

Balsamic Onions

1 tablespoon **oil**

2 **onions**, cut into wedges

1 tablespoon **balsamic vinegar**

1 tablespoon **brown sugar**

Mash

4 medium **potatoes**, peeled

1" cube of **butter**

salt and **pepper**

2 **steaks**, either fillet, topside or rump, about 1" thick

oil to fry

---

1. To make the mustard sauce, simply mix the crème fraîche and mustard together. Leave in the fridge until needed.

2. To make the balsamic onions, heat the oil in a pan and add the onions. Cook until they become quite brown; the caramelization of the onions adds to the flavour. This may take 4 - 5 minutes. Stir frequently.

3. Once the onions are browned, add the balsamic vinegar and sugar and season well. Bring to the boil, turn down the heat and simmer for 2 - 3 minutes. Leave to stand until needed.

4. Make the mashed potatoes (see page 19). Once done, leave in the pan, with the lid on until needed.

5. Heat a little oil in a frying pan. Have the heat quite high and when the oil begins to have a heat haze above it, (it does not need to smoke) add the steaks.

6. For a rare steak, cook on this high heat for 2 minutes each side, turn down to a medium heat and cook for a further 2 minutes each side.

7. For a medium steak, cook on this high heat for 2 minutes each side, turn down to a medium heat and cook for a further 4 minutes each side.

8. For a well done steak, cook on this high heat for 2 minutes each side, turn down to a medium heat and cook for a further 6 minutes each side.

9. Serve the steak with the mash, balsamic onions and the mustard sauce.

NOTE: Many students have asked me how to cook a steak. Here is the classic. After a few tries you will discover whether you like your steak rare, medium or well done.

TIP: Fillet steaks are probably the most foolproof to do, but the most expensive.

TIP: The above timings are for a 1" thick steak, but if the steak is thinner cook for less time.

Saffron Ginger Chicken
with rice and naan bread

8 **chicken thighs**

3 tablespoons grated **fresh ginger**

4 cloves **garlic**, finely chopped

juice of a **lemon**

1 teaspoon **paprika**

1 teaspoon ground **coriander**

1 tablespoon **oil**

2 **onions**, cut into wedges

1 x 400ml can **coconut milk**

1 good pinch of **saffron** or 1 teaspoon **turmeric**

1 fat **red chilli**, deseeded and cut into slices

1 teaspoon **liquid chicken stock** or ½ **stock cube**

1 tablespoon chopped **fresh coriander**

2 mugs **rice**

1 mug **peas**

4 **naan breads**

1. Put the chicken in a bowl with the ginger, garlic, lemon, paprika and ground coriander. Leave overnight if possible. A minimum of one hour is OK.

2. Heat the oil in a wok and fry the onions. Take the chicken from the marinade and fry until the meat is browned. Add the coconut milk, saffron, chilli, stock and the marinade juices. Bring to the boil, then turn down to simmer with a lid on, for 40 minutes. Stir occasionally. Add the coriander just before serving.

3. While the chicken is cooking, put 4 mugs of water in a saucepan. Bring to the boil and add the rice. Bring back to the boil, then turn down to simmer, with the lid on, for 10 minutes or until all the water is absorbed.

4. After the rice has been cooking for 7 minutes, add the peas on top.

5. Heat the naan breads according to the instructions on the pack.

6. Serve with a little yogurt.

NOTE: This chicken recipe is so fragrant and spicy. The slow cook method produces lovely tender chicken.

TIP: To deseed a chilli without cutting it in half, simply cut off the stalk end and gently roll between your hands. The seeds should fall out, giving you seed-free rings when chopped.

Italian Meatballs
with spaghetti

Tomato Sauce

oil to fry

1 **onion** finely chopped

1 clove **garlic**, finely chopped

1 x 400g **tin tomatoes**

1 tablespoon **tomato purée**

1 tablespoon **brown sugar**

1 tablespoon **wine vinegar**

1 tablespoon **fresh basil, chopped**

½ mug **water**

salt and **pepper**

½ x 500g pack **spaghetti**

Meatballs

250g **beef mince**

½ small **onion**, finely chopped

salt and **pepper**

oil to fry

Garnish - 1 tablespoon chopped **fresh basil** (pictured - coriander).

1. To make the sauce, heat a little oil in a saucepan and fry the onion and garlic for 2 - 3 minutes. Add the rest of the sauce ingredients, bring to the boil, then turn down to simmer for 5 minutes.

2. Once cooked, blitz with a hand-held blender.

3. In a mixing bowl, combine the beef, onion and seasoning together with your hands and make as smooth as possible.

4. Take a dessertspoonful of mixture and form into balls and set aside. The mixture should make about 16 meatballs.

5. Put the spaghetti on to boil (see page 22).

6. Heat about ½" of oil in the bottom of a frying pan. When the oil makes the meatballs sizzle (test one), add the meatballs to the pan. As they begin to brown, turn them so all sides become browned. Once cooked, take from the pan and drain on some kitchen paper.

7. Drain the spaghetti.

8. Add the meatballs and sauce to the spaghetti and mix. Garnish with basil and serve.

NOTE: A little time consuming, but well worth the effort. Making meatballs from fresh ingredients produces a great beefy flavour. The piquant tomato sauce is yummy.

Sweet and Sour Fish
with coconut rice and mangetout

Sauce

3 tablespoons **tomato purée**

1 heaped tablespoon **honey**

4 tablespoons **white wine vinegar**

2 tablespoons **soy sauce**

1 tablespoon freshly grated **ginger**

1 **onion**, chopped

a little **oil** to fry

2 pieces of **cod** or **haddock**

1 mug **rice**

1 x 400g tin **coconut milk**

12 pieces of **mangetout**, sliced lengthways

1. Preheat the oven to 190°C fan oven/210°C/Gas 6.

2. To make the sauce, fry the onion and ginger in the oil until the onion begins to soften. Add the rest of the sauce ingredients and bring to the boil. Take off the heat. The mixture should be quite thick.

3. Place the fish in a greased casserole dish and spread the sauce over the top. Bake in the oven for 15 - 20 minutes, depending on the thickness of the fish. If the fish is 1" thick, cook for 15 minutes, if it is 1½" thick for 20 minutes.

4. Whilst the fish is in the oven, cook the rice. Use the coconut milk and make it up to 2 mugs worth of liquid by adding water. Bring to the boil in a saucepan and then add the rice. Stir once and bring back to the boil. Turn down to simmer and put a lid on the pan. 3 minutes before the end of the cooking time, add the sliced mangetout on top and replace the lid. Once cooked, stir together.

5. Serve the fish on top of the rice.

NOTE: The lovely, light, delicate flavours in this dish go well with the coconut rice.

Seafood and Spinach Pasta
with salmon and prawns

1 mug **fusilli** (name for twirly pasta)

6 pieces of **frozen spinach**, defrosted and drained of most of the water.

1 mug grated **cheddar**

plus ½ mug grated **cheese for sprinkling** over the top

1 tablespoon **flour**

1½ mug **milk**

1" cube **butter**

¼ teaspoon **paprika**

2 small pieces of **salmon steak**, cut into chunks

10 large **prawns**

2 **spring onions**, chopped

4 **mushrooms**, sliced

1. Preheat the oven to 180ºC fan oven/200ºC/Gas 6. Grease an ovenproof dish or individual dishes.

2. Boil water in a saucepan for the pasta. Once boiling, add the pasta and cook for approximately 10 minutes, or until tender. Once cooked, drain and stir in the spinach. Set aside in a bowl until needed.

3. Put one mug of the grated cheese into a saucepan and add the flour. Mix evenly. Add the milk and butter and heat gently. Stir all the time and the sauce will thicken. Add the paprika and stir.

4. Put the salmon, prawns, chopped spring onions and mushrooms in the cheese sauce and stir. Add the cooked pasta and spinach. Pour into a casserole dish or individual dishes.

5. Sprinkle the ½ mug of cheese over the top.

6. Bake in the oven for 25 minutes. The top should be browned.

NOTE: A very 'moreish' combination of salmon and prawns, with a delicate cheese sauce.

TIP: Here we have made the one pot into three, but of course you can easily make it into one!

Crispy Fried Duck Breast
with ginger dressing and fried rice

1 mug **basmati rice**

2 medium **carrots**, diced into small pieces

1 **courgette**, diced into small pieces

2 **duck breasts**

2 **eggs**, beaten

2 **spring onions**, chopped

Dressing

1 tablespoon **oil**

3 **spring onions**, chopped finely

1 tablespoon freshly grated **ginger**

juice of 1 **lime**

2 tablespoons **soy sauce**

1 tablespoon **honey**

1. Put 2 mugs of water in a saucepan and bring to the boil. Add the rice and the carrots. Bring back to the boil and turn down to simmer with the lid on, for 10 minutes. Add the courgettes on top of the rice. No need to stir them in. Replace the pan lid and cook for a further 5 minutes.

2. To make the dressing, heat a little oil in a pan and fry the spring onions and ginger for 30 seconds. Add the rest of the dressing ingredients and cook for another 30 seconds. Set aside until needed.

3. Score (make incisions with a sharp knife) the duck breast with a knife, as this will allow the fat to come out of the skin whilst it is cooking.

4. Heat some oil in a frying pan. Fry the duck breasts on a high heat for 2 minutes each side. Turn down the heat and cook, with the skin side down and with a lid on the pan, for a further 8 minutes.

5. Once the duck breast is cooked, take out of the frying pan and leave to rest while you fry the rice.

6. Add a little oil to a clean frying pan. Pour in the beaten egg, allow it to spread over the bottom of the pan. Once cooked, take out of the pan and cut into strips.

7. Add a little more oil to the pan and fry the spring onions for 30 seconds. Stir the egg and onions into the cooked rice mixture.

8. Serve the duck breast on the rice and pour the dressing over.

NOTE: Cooked this way, the duck breast stays really tender. The ginger sauce is fragrant and sophisticated. An ideal meal to cook for guests.

Tim's Slow Cooked Shepherd's Pie
with sweet potato topping

oil to fry

1 onion, chopped

750g pack diced lamb

1 tablespoon flour

2 carrots, chopped

2 mugs water

1 tablespoon liquid vegetable stock

2 sprigs rosemary

Mash Topping

4 medium potatoes, peeled and cut into chunks

3 medium sweet potatoes, peeled and cut into chunks

2 x 1" cubes of butter

salt and pepper

1 egg, beaten

---

1. Preheat the oven to 180°C fan oven/200°C/Gas 6.

2. Heat a little oil in a pan. Add the onions and fry until they become soft.

3. Add the meat and cook until no longer pink. Add the flour and stir.

4. Add the carrots, water and stock and bring to the boil. Season well with salt and pepper and add the rosemary sprigs.

5. Transfer the meat into a casserole dish. Cover the dish and place in the oven for 1 hour.

6. Check the casserole, if it is looking a little dry just add more water.

7. Turn down the oven to 160°C fan oven/180°C/Gas 4 and cook for a further 2½ hours.

8. Put some water on to boil and add the potatoes. Simmer for 15 minutes or until tender.

9. Once cooked, add the butter to the potatoes, season well and mash.

10. Check the casserole again and add more water if necessary. The gravy should be as thick as double cream. Put the mashed potatoes on top and brush with the beaten egg. Turn the oven back up to 180°C fan/200°C/gas 6 and put the pie in for 25 - 30 minutes. The top should be browned.

11. Serve with peas.

NOTE: This is one of Tim's contributions to the book. He wanted to produce the best Shepherd's Pie he could. The result is this delicious slow cooked lamb, with yummy gravy and mixed potato topping.

TIP: Make sure that the gravy has not dried up too much before adding the potato topping. Just add a little more water if necessary.

Irish Lamb Stew
with colcannon

Oil for frying

2 **onions**, sliced

2 cloves **garlic**, finely chopped

750g **stewing lamb**

4 **carrots**, chopped

1 tablespoon **flour**

1 mug **water** + tablespoon **concentrated vegetable stock**, or a **stock cube**

2 tablespoons **apricot jam**

1 mug **red wine**

1 sprig of **rosemary**, left whole

5 - 6 **mushrooms**, halved

Colcannon

6 medium **potatoes**, peeled and cut into chunks

50g **butter**

250g pack of **spring greens** or **savoy cabbage**, chopped

½ x 300ml pot of **soured cream**

1. Preheat the oven to 180ºC fan oven/200ºC/ Gas 6.

2. Heat the oil in a large saucepan or 'hob to oven' casserole. Fry the onions and garlic until the onions are soft.

3. Add the meat and the carrots and fry until the meat is no longer pink.

4. Add the flour and mix well. Cook for 1 minute until everything is coated in the flour.

5. Add the water, stock, apricot jam, wine and rosemary. Stir well. The sauce in the casserole should thicken.

6. Add the mushrooms.

7. If you have not used a 'hob to oven' casserole dish, pour the contents of the pan into a casserole dish and cover with a lid or foil. Place in the oven for 1½ hours. Stir half way through the cooking time.

8. To make the Colcannon, put the potatoes in boiling water and simmer gently for 10 - 15 minutes until tender. Drain and mash the potatoes and mix in the soured cream. Heat the butter in a wok or large frying pan and fry the spring greens for 2 - 3 minutes. Stir the cabbage into the potatoes and season well with salt and pepper.

NOTE: Colcannon is Irish mashed potatoes, they are really tasty and easy to do. You can of course replace them with normal mash or roast potatoes.

TIP: Don't forget the rule of cooking with alcohol: "If it's not good enough to drink, it's not good enough to cook with".

Sweet Honey Chicken
with risotto rice

Marinade

2 tablespoons **soy sauce**

2 tablespoons fresh grated **ginger**

2 tablespoons **honey**

1 dessertspoon dried **chives**

2 **chicken breasts**

Risotto rice

25g of **butter** - measure by the packet markings

1 clove **garlic**, finely chopped

1 **yellow pepper**, chopped

1 mug **basmati rice**

2 mugs **water**

1 teaspoon **liquid chicken stock** or ½ a **stock cube**

2 **mushrooms**, sliced

4 **spring onions**, chopped

1 **courgette**, cut into small chunks

---

1. In a big bowl mix the chicken breast and the marinade ingredients together. Leave for about half an hour. If you don't have the time, 10 minutes will do.

2. Prepare the risotto rice. Melt the butter in a saucepan and add the garlic and peppers. Cook for 2 minutes, taking care not to burn the butter. Add the rice and cook for 1 minute, allowing the liquid to absorb the rice.

3. Add the water and stock, stir well and bring to the boil. Once boiling, turn down the heat and simmer for 10 minutes. Stir occasionally.

4. After 10 minutes, add the mushrooms, spring onions and courgettes. Cook for a further 5 minutes. Stir occasionally and add more water if necessary. Risotto should not be dry but have a creamy consistency.

5. While the risotto is cooking, heat a little oil in a frying pan. Remove the chicken from the marinade (don't throw the marinade away) and cook the chicken on a high heat for 2 minutes each side.

6. Add the rest of the marinade and turn down the heat. Cook, with the lid on, for a further 4 - 6 minutes, depending on the thickness of the chicken.

7. Test that the chicken is cooked all the way through by cutting through the middle of one. If cooked, take the chicken out and cut into slices. If the sauce has not thickened, simmer gently for a few minutes.

8. Serve the chicken on top of the risotto rice and spoon over the sauce.

NOTE: Delicious, sweet and savoury chicken dish. Easy and quick to make.

TIP: If you plan to eat this when you return home from work, marinate the chicken overnight in the fridge.

TIP: You can use this risotto rice with other dishes to make a change.

One-Pot Cooking

Why is one-pot cooking so popular? Less washing up? Simple recipes? Quick to make? Whatever it is, this section has some one-pot recipes for you. Some of the recipes are quick to make and some might take a little longer, but all deliver hearty main meals. You will enjoy this section a lot more if you get yourself a 'hob to oven' casserole dish.

Veggie Stew
with suet dumplings

1 tablespoon **oil** to fry

1 red **onion**, chopped

1 clove **garlic**, finely chopped

2 **carrots**, cut into rings

2 **celery** sticks, sliced

1 **sweet potato**, peeled and cut into chunks

10 - 12 **green beans**, cut into ½" pieces

5 **mushrooms**, sliced

1 **courgette**, cut into small chunks

1 tablespoon **Worcestershire sauce** (don't use if you are serving vegetarians)

3 mugs **water**

1 **veggie stock pot** or 1 tablespoon **concentrated vegetable stock**

1 tablespoon freshly chopped **basil**

salt and **pepper**

Dumplings

½ mug **suet**

1 mug **self-raising flour**

¼ mug **water**

¼ teaspoon **salt**

---

1. Make the dumplings by mixing together the flour, salt and suet in a bowl. Add the water and it should make a soft dough. Make approximately 9 small balls. Set to one side until needed.

2. Heat a little oil in a large frying pan and fry the onions, garlic, carrots and celery until the onions are soft.

3. Add the sweet potato, mushrooms and green beans. Fry for 2 - 3 minutes.

4. Add the stock, water and Worcestershire sauce and bring to the boil. Season well with salt and pepper and simmer for 10 minutes.

5. Add the courgettes and the dumplings and simmer with the lid on the pan for another 10 minutes.

6. Add the fresh herbs just before serving.

NOTE: This is a delightful vegetarian meal. Very easy and quick to prepare. As the vegetables cook together, they produce a delicious soup.

| £3.05 /PERSON | EASE ★★ | SERVES 2 | PREP 25 MINS |

Five Spice Beef Noodles
with hoisin sauce

1 tablespoon **oil**

350g **rump, sirloin or topside beef**, cut into thin strips

½ **onion**, sliced

1 small **red or green pepper**, thinly sliced

1 teaspoon grated fresh **ginger**

1 clove **garlic**

6 **mushrooms**, sliced

½ teaspoon **'five spice' powder**

1 x pack fresh or **ready-to-wok egg noodles**.

Sauce

¼ mug **hoisin sauce**

1 tablespoon **soy sauce**

1 tablespoon **wine vinegar**

1 tablespoon **water**

1. Heat the oil in a wok. Add the beef strips and cook on high heat for 2 - 3 minutes. Remove from the pan and set to one side.

2. Add the onions, garlic, peppers and ginger to the pan. Stir fry for 1 - 2 minutes on high heat.

3. Add the mushrooms and the five spice powder. Cook for 1 minute on high heat.

4. Return the beef to the pan with the sauce ingredients and the noodles. Cook on high heat for 1 minute until everything is heated through.

5. Serve immediately.

NOTE: Tasty and filling stir fry, with a delicious gingery sauce.

TIP: Rump steak is expensive, but you do not need a lot for this recipe. Cut it very thinly for the best results.

Chorizo and Butter Bean Stew
with crusty bread

1 small **onion**, sliced

½ **red pepper**, sliced

400g tin **butter beans**, rinsed and drained

4 **mushrooms**, sliced

2 medium sized **chorizo sausages**, cut into thin slices

1 tablespoon **balsamic vinegar**

½ mug **water**

1 tablespoon concentrated **liquid chicken stock**

1 teaspoon **sugar**

crusty bread to serve.

1. Heat a little oil in a wok and fry the chorizo for 2 - 3 minutes. Remove from the pan and set to one side. Tip out most of the fat, leaving approximately 1 tablespoon in the pan.

2. Add the peppers and onions to the wok and fry until they begin to soften.

3. Add the mushrooms, stock, water, balsamic vinegar and sugar. Return the chorizo to the pan and bring to the boil. Turn down to simmer for 4 - 5 minutes.

4. Add the beans to the pan and boil for 1 minute.

5. Eat with the crusty bread.

NOTE: The spicy chorizo and the butter beans make a great combination, along with the bitter sweet sauce.

WHERE ON EARTH: Chorizo sausages are often with the cooked meats, or on the deli counter.

£1.80 /PERSON | EASE ★ | SERVES 2 | PREP 25 MINS

Sweet and Sour Chicken Noodles
with a honey and ginger sauce

4 **spring onions**, chopped

½ **red pepper**, chopped

1 clove **garlic**, finely chopped

1 **chicken breast**, cut into thin slices

½ x 400g pack of **fresh egg noodles** or **straight-to-wok noodles**

oil to fry

Sauce

2 tablespoons **tomato purée**

1 tablespoon **honey**

3 tablespoons **white wine vinegar**

1 tablespoon **soy sauce**

1 tablespoon grated fresh **ginger**

6 - 7 tablespoons **water**

1. Heat the oil in a wok, add the onions, peppers and garlic, fry for 1 minute.

2. Add the chicken and cook until no longer pink.

3. Mix the sauce ingredients together and add. Cook until it bubbles.

4. Add the noodles. Cook for 1 minute, stirring well to mix everything together.

5. Eat immediately!

NOTE: An easy to make noodle dish, with a lovely piquant honey and ginger sauce.

WHERE ON EARTH: Wine vinegars are sometimes found near the pickles, above the frozen foods in the supermarket.

Chicken Biryani
with naan bread

2 x 1" cube **butter**

1 medium **onion**, cut into wedges

4 boneless **chicken thighs**

4 tablespoons **korma curry paste**

1 teaspoon **turmeric** or 1 pinch of **saffron**

1 mug **rice**

1 teaspoon **liquid chicken stock** or ½ **stock cube**

1 mug **yogurt**

⅓ mug **raisins**

2 mugs **water**

1 tablespoon chopped fresh **coriander leaves**

¼ mug toasted, **flaked almonds**

2 **naan breads**

1. Heat the butter in a large pan or wok and cook the onions until they become soft. Add the chicken and cook until the skins have browned a little.

2. Add the korma paste and turmeric or saffron and cook for 1 minute.

3. Add the rice and stir well. Cook for 1 minute, allowing the rice to absorb the flavours.

4. Add the stock, yogurt, raisins and water. Bring to the boil. Turn down and simmer with the lid on for 25 - 30 minutes. Check every 10 minutes to make sure it is not sticking to the bottom. You may need to add a little more water. Try not to stir too much as the rice will become mushy.

5. At the end of the cooking time, add the coriander leaves and the almonds, stirring as little as possible. Do not cook any more.

6. Serve with warm naan breads.

NOTE: This biryani is delicious. Its subtle spicing is a winner. An easy one-pot dish.

Thai Salmon
with coconut rice and green chilli dressing

2 tablespoons **olive oil**

2 tablespoons **Thai red curry paste**

4 **spring onions**, chopped

400g can **coconut milk**

½ mug **water**

1 tablespoon **chopped fresh coriander leaves**

grated zest of a **lemon**

1 mug **rice**

2 **salmon steaks**

Dressing

juice of a **lemon**

1 tablespoon **hoisin sauce**

1 teaspoon **sugar**

3 **spring onions**, chopped

1 fat **green chilli**, cut into rings

1. Heat a little oil in a frying pan or large saucepan, add the curry paste and fry for 30 seconds, stirring all the time. Add the spring onions and fry for another 30 seconds.

2. Add the coconut milk, water, chopped coriander and lemon zest.

3. Once boiling, add the rice and bring back to the point of simmering.

4. Place the salmon steaks on the top of the rice. It doesn't matter if they sink down into the liquid a little, the rice will soon absorb the liquid. Turn the heat down low and cover the pan with a lid or foil. Cook for 10 - 15 minutes.

5. While the fish is cooking, make the dressing by just mixing the ingredients together in a bowl.

6. Once the rice and fish are cooked, serve the rice with the fish on top and drizzle the dressing over.

NOTE: Lovely and spicy, but does not overwhelm the salmon. The coconut rice is delightful.

WHERE ON EARTH: Thai red curry paste is often in the 'overseas' section or with the other Oriental sauces.

One Pot Pork Chop Roast
with bacon and apple

4 good sized **pork chops**

2 red **eating apples**, cored and cut into chunks

1 clove **garlic**, chopped

8 **rashers of bacon**, cut into strips

2 **onions**, cut into wedges

4 - 5 medium **potatoes**, cut into 2" chunks

a few sprigs of **rosemary**

1 mug **cider**

salt and **pepper**

Gravy

1 **onion**, sliced

1 tablespoon **oil**

1 dessertspoon **flour**

1 mug **cider**

1 tablespoon **concentrated vegetable stock**, or one **stock cube**

1. Preheat the oven to 180°C fan oven/200°C/Gas 6.

2. Place the chops, apples, garlic, bacon, onions and potatoes in a large, greased roasting tin or casserole dish. Sprinkle with oil, salt and pepper. Mix together.

3. Nestle the chops under the vegetables, as this will stop them becoming too dry. Sprinkle over the rosemary. Pour over the mug of cider and season well. Place in the oven for 45 minutes.

4. While the dish is cooking, make the gravy. Fry the onion in a little oil until it is quite browned. Add the flour and cook for 30 seconds. Add the cider and the stock, so the gravy should thicken a little. Season well. You can serve this gravy as it is or blitz with a hand-held blender.

NOTE: This is so quick and easy to prepare. The classic pork and apple combination does not fail to please.

TIP: Make sure that the flesh of the pork is nestled into the ingredients well and that the fat is left out to brown.

TIP: You'll only need one can or bottle of cider for this recipe. Try not to get cheap and nasty stuff. The rule when using alcohol in cooking is "If it's not good enough to drink, it's not good enough to cook with".

Slow Cook Beef Hot Pot
with yummy sliced potatoes

1 tablespoon **oil**

2 **onions**, sliced

2 cloves **garlic**, finely chopped

400g **stewing steak**

1 tablespoon **flour**

2 mugs **water**

1 **beef stock cube**, or **stock pot** or 1 **tablespoon liquid stock**

3 - 4 **carrots**, sliced

4 - 5 **mushrooms**, sliced

6 medium **potatoes**, sliced into ¼" slices

salt and **pepper**

---

1. Preheat the oven to 180ºC fan oven/200ºC/Gas 6.

2. Heat the oil in a 'hob to oven' casserole dish or large pan. Add the onions and garlic and fry until they become soft.

3. Add the meat and cook until it is browned a little.

4. Add the flour and cook for 1 minute, making sure that the flour is evenly distributed.

5. Add the water and the stock cube and bring to the boil, stirring well.

6. Add the carrots and mushrooms. Season with salt and pepper. The sauce should thicken slightly.

7. If you are not using a 'hob to oven' casserole, pour the contents of the pan into a large casserole dish.

8. Arrange the sliced potatoes over the top. Season well. Cover with a lid or foil and place in the oven for 1¼ hours.

9. Take the lid or foil off the casserole and continue to cook for a further 30 minutes. The potatoes should be browned on the top.

NOTE: Tender stewed beef and vegetables, along with roasted potatoes on the top, is almost comfort food.

TIP: This is a great recipe to cook at the weekend and freeze half of it for a meal during the week.

TIP: Getting a 'hob to oven' pan or casserole dish is a great investment. Basically a 'hob to oven' pan is just a pan that has metal handles and an oven proof lid. Obviously plastic handles wouldn't like going into the oven too much! A good one should last most of your life.

Light and Lemony Prawn Risotto
with arborio rice

50g (⅕ x 250g block) cube **butter**

1 **onion**, chopped

½ **red pepper**, chopped quite small

1 mug **risotto (arborio) rice**

2 mugs **water**

1 **vegetable stock cube**

1 x 400g pack of **cooked prawns**

½ x 340g tin **sweetcorn**

1 tablespoon **chopped fresh chives**

juice of a **lemon**

1. Heat the butter in a frying pan and add the onion. Fry until the onion and pepper begins to soften. Keep the heat fairly high, but be careful not to burn the butter.

2. Add the risotto rice and cook until it absorbs the butter, approximately 1 minute.

3. Add the water and stock cube and bring to the boil. Once boiling, turn down the heat and simmer with no lid on, for 12 - 15 minutes until the rice is tender. It may be necessary to add a little more water. Risotto should not be dry, but have a creamy consistency. The prawns will produce some liquid, so allow for that.

4. Add the prawns and sweetcorn, cook for 1 minute on a medium heat. Add the chives and lemon juice, cook for 30 seconds. This should be enough to heat the prawns through.

5. Eat straight away.

NOTE: Fantastic, fresh and light risotto. Very easy to make.

£2.00 /PERSON

EASE ★

SERVES 2-3

PREP 20 MINS

COOK 20 MINS

One-Pot Pancetta Risotto
with mushrooms and tomatoes

oil to fry

250g pack of **pancetta lardons**

1 **onion**, chopped

1 clove **garlic**, finely chopped

1 mug **basmati rice**

2 mugs **water**

1 **chicken stock pot** or 1 tablespoon **concentrated chicken stock**

4 - 5 **mushrooms**, sliced

1 teaspoon **mixed dried herbs**

250g pack **cherry tomatoes**, each one halved

½ mug freshly grated **Parmesan** cheese

pepper to season

1. Preheat the oven to 180°C fan oven/200°C/Gas 6.

2. Heat a small amount of oil in a 'hob to oven' pan or casserole and fry the bacon lardons. Cook until they become browned and crisp.

3. Add the onions and garlic and cook until the onions become soft.

4. Add the rice to the pan and cook for 1 minute until the rice has absorbed the liquid in the pan.

5. Add the water and the stock. Bring to the boil, stirring frequently. Season with pepper, the bacon will provide enough saltiness.

6. Take off the heat and add the mushrooms, herbs and tomatoes. Mix together.

7. Cover with a lid or foil and place in the oven for 25 - 30 minutes until the rice is cooked.

8. Take out of the oven and stir in the Parmesan cheese.

NOTE: The Parmesan, bacon and tomatoes in this recipe make for a very appealing meal.

TIP: If you do not have an ovenproof pan, just start the cooking in a normal pan and transfer to a casserole dish when you put the risotto in the oven.

Comfort Food

Had a hard week at work? Bad day with your boss? Feeling overworked, underpaid, not valued? Days when everything goes wrong and you want something to make you feel warm and fuzzy inside, all you need is something indulgent, pampering and soothing. Here's the section just for you.

Mars bars are supposed to help you 'work, rest and play'. I have included a wonderful Mars Bar Munchie recipe which is very naughty, but very nice and very delicious. Here, there are some good alternatives to curling up with a tub of ice cream and a spoon.

Mars Bar Munchies
with lots of crunch and naughtiness

1½ x 300g packs of **Hob Nob biscuits**

5 x regular size (58g) **Mars bars**

½ mug **sugar**

1 tablespoon **golden syrup**

250g **milk chocolate**, measure by the packet

1 mug **double cream**

150g block **white chocolate**

---

1. Line a regular 18 x 27 cm baking tray with greaseproof paper.

2. Put the biscuits in a poly bag. Crush them with a rolling pin or other implement, making sure you leave some quite big pieces in there to add some crunch to your Munchies.

3. Cut the Mars bars into ¼" chunks. Mix with the crushed biscuits.

4. Put the sugar, syrup, milk chocolate and cream into a mixing bowl resting over the top of a pan of simmering water. Heat gently until everything is smooth and the chocolate is dissolved. Take off the heat and allow to cool for 4 - 5 minutes.

5. Add to the crushed biscuits and Mars bars and mix well. Don't stir them too much, as they need to stay whole and not melt into the rest of the chocolate.

6. Turn the mixture out into the baking tray and spread it evenly across the tray with the back of a metal spoon.

7. Melt the chocolate (see page 18).

8. Using a metal spoon, drizzle over the Munchies in a decorative manner. See photo.

9. Leave the Munchies in the fridge for 2 - 3 hours. Take out of the tray, remove the greaseproof paper and cut into small squares.

NOTE: An absolute favourite with almost everyone who tries these little treats, but just a little naughty. Make sure you cut these up into small squares and savour them. It is best if you make these when friends are around, otherwise, you'll end up eating them all yourself!

Cinnamon Swirls
with puff pastry

1 x 375g pack of **ready-rolled puff pastry**

1 tablespoon **apricot jam**

2 tablespoons **sugar**

1 teaspoon **cinnamon**

1. Preheat the oven to 200°C fan oven/220°C/Gas 7. Prepare a well-greased non-stick baking tray (see note below).

2. Flatten out the rolled pastry. Spread the jam evenly over it. Mix together the cinnamon and sugar in a small bowl and sprinkle over the jam.

3. With the shortest side of the pastry closest to you, cut into three horizontally and then cut vertically down the middle, giving you 6 squares. Cut each square in half diagonally, giving you 12 triangles. Roll them up across from one point to another. Place on the baking sheet.

4. Place in the oven for 10 minutes. Remove from the baking sheet before any spilled jam or sugar has time to set.

NOTE: These are quick and easy to make. Great when friends drop in. When eaten warm, the crunchy, fresh pastry, along with the sweetness of the jam and spiciness of the cinnamon, is yummy!

TIP: You can buy, for about £4, amazing things called reusable Teflon non-stick baking sheets (found near the cling film in the supermarket). They are perfect for this recipe as the swirls will pretty much never stick. All you need to do is rinse the baking sheet in soapy water and it should come clean easily; you will then be able to use it again another day.

WHERE ON EARTH: You will find the puff pastry in the 'frozen food' section near the desserts.

Chocolate fridge cake
with orange and figs

1. Grease and line an 8" loose bottomed cake tin.

2. Place the butter and the chocolate in a mixing bowl, resting it over a pan of gently boiling water and allow to melt. Stir every now and then.

3. While the chocolate is melting, put the biscuits in a plastic bag and gently bash them with a rolling pin or similar implement. Keep them fairly rustic, don't beat them to dust.

4. Remove the stalky bit from the figs and cut the rest quite finely.

5. Once the chocolate has melted, take off the heat. Add the crème fraîche and stir until it has melted into the chocolate.

6. Add the figs and orange rind and stir.

7. Add the biscuit bits to the chocolate mixture and gently combine. The mixture will still be quite runny. Pour into the prepared cake tin and place in the fridge for a minimum of 3 hours, preferably overnight.

8. Serve in small portions with coffee.

⅗ x 250g block **butter**

200g **milk chocolate**

100g **dark chocolate**

½ x 250g packet of **ready-to-eat figs**

¾ x 300g pack of **Hob Nob biscuits**

1 x 250 ml pot of **crème fraîche**

grated rind of 2 **oranges**

NOTE: This is a very rich cake, so you only need small portions for each person. If you don't like figs you can replace them with any other dried fruits, apricots, raisins, etc; make sure they are the ready-to-eat variety and quite soft.

Do-It-Yourself Jaffa Cakes
great to share

1. Preheat the oven to 200°C fan oven/220°C/Gas 7. Grease 2 large baking trays and line with greaseproof paper.

2. Whisk the eggs and sugar until they are thick and creamy in colour.

3. Add the orange rind and the flour and fold in gently.

4. Place small rounds of the mixture, spaced well apart, on the baking trays. Should make between 20 - 30.

5. Place in the oven for 8 minutes or until golden brown.

6. Cool slightly and then take the biscuits off the greaseproof paper.

7. Once cool, turn upside down and place a small blob of orange marmalade on each one.

8. Melt the chocolate (see page 18). Place about 1 teaspoon of chocolate on each cake and spread around. Leave until the chocolate is set.

2 **eggs**

3 tablespoons **caster sugar**

grated rind of an **orange**

4 tablespoons **self-raising flour**

250g **dark chocolate**

orange marmalade

NOTE: Taste and look very much like Jaffa cakes, but are fun to make, especially with friends.

Carrot cake
with creamy topping

5 - 6 medium **carrots**, sliced

4 **eggs**, whites and yolks separated

200g **butter**, melted

grated rind and juice of 1 **orange**

¾ mug **sugar**

1 teaspoon **cinnamon**

2 mugs **self-raising flour**

Topping

100g softened **butter** (see tip)

1½ mugs **icing sugar**

1 teaspoon **vanilla extract**

---

1. Preheat the oven to 180°C fan oven/200°C/Gas 6. Grease and line the bottom of a 23 cm/9" cake tin.

2. Boil the carrots for 15 minutes, drain and roughly mash, allow to cool a little.

3. Put the carrots, egg yolks, melted butter, orange juice, orange rind, sugar, cinnamon and flour in a large bowl and mix well.

4. Whisk the egg whites until they are stiff enough to form soft peaks.

5. Fold ½ the egg whites into the carrot mixture, once the mixture is smooth, gently fold in the rest of the egg whites. (See page 15)

6. Pour into the cake tin. Place in the oven for 35 - 40 minutes until the cakes "bounce back" when gently pressed.

7. Make the butter cream filling by creaming the ingredients together. Spread over the top of the cake, once the cake has come out of the oven and cooled.

NOTE: A really delightful, moist, carrot cake ,with a simple butter and sugar topping.

TIP: You could also make this into small cakes, put in cake cases and only cook for 15 - 20 minutes. One option is to replace the butter cream filling with whipped cream.

TIP: Softened butter is just butter left at room temperature; it just makes it easier to work with.

Almond and Pecan Cookies
with orange and almonds

1. Preheat the oven to 160°C fan oven/180°C/Gas 4.

2. Beat together the butter and sugar with electric beaters or a wooden spoon, until light and fluffy. Add the egg yolk and vanilla extract. Beat together.

3. Add the rest of the ingredients and mix together with a metal spoon. The mixture will be quite stiff.

4. Turn out onto a floured board and press together. Form into 2 long, fat sausage shapes (around 25 cm/10" long).

5. Cover with cling film and allow to rest in the fridge for 45 minutes.

6. Grease a couple of baking sheets. Cut the 'sausages' into 12 biscuits each.

7. Place the biscuit sections directly onto the baking trays, put in the oven for 15 - 20 minutes until they begin to brown.

250g block **butter**, room temperature

¾ mug **caster sugar**

1 **egg yolk**

1 teaspoon **vanilla extract**

2 mugs **plain flour**

75g pack of **flaked almonds**

½ mug **chopped pecan nuts**

grated rind of a small **orange**

NOTE: Lovely crunchy, buttery cookies. Will keep in a tin for a few days if you hide them!

Mocha Cookies
great after dinner, or with coffee

1. Preheat the oven to 160°C fan oven/180°C/Gas 4. Lightly grease 2 baking trays.

2. Cream together the butter and sugar with a wooden spoon or electric beaters, until light and fluffy.

3. Add the egg yolk, melted chocolate, milk and instant coffee. Beat together.

4. Using a metal spoon, stir in the flour.

5. Place teaspoon-sized blobs on the baking trays. Place in the oven for 10 minutes.

6. Remove from the oven and make indents in the cookies with the handle of a wooden spoon while the cookies are still warm. This makes a small 'well' to hold the white chocolate.

7. Melt the white chocolate (see page 18). Once the cookies have cooled, fill the wells with the white chocolate.

175g softened **butter**

¾ mug **caster sugar**

1 **egg yolk**

100g bar **chocolate**, melted

1 dessertspoon **milk**

1 dessertspoon **instant coffee granules**

1½ mugs **plain flour**

200g bar **white chocolate** for decoration

Chocolate Fruit Crunchies
with blueberries

100g block **dark chocolate**

50g **butter**

2 tablespoons **golden syrup**

75g pack of **dried blueberries**

2½ mugs **cornflakes**

12 cake cases

---

1. Put the chocolate, butter and syrup in a large saucepan and heat gently.

2. Once everything is melted and well mixed, add the blueberries. Then add the cornflakes and stir well.

3. Divide between the 12 cake cases and leave to cool in the fridge for about 1 hour.

NOTE: These are just a little different from the ones you may have made as a child. The dark chocolate and the tangy fruit in them give a hint of being grown up! You can of course revert back to milk chocolate and add any kind of dried fruit or nuts. Very easy to experiment with.

Nut and Chocolate Slices
with almonds and pistachios

125g **dark chocolate**

⅕ x 250g block **butter**

1 **egg** white

½ mug **caster sugar**

½ x 100g pack **ground almonds**

½ x 100g pack **pistachio nuts**, chopped

½ x 100g pack toasted **flaked almonds**

1. Melt the chocolate and the butter in a bowl, over a pan of simmering water (see page 18). Set to one side.

2. Whisk the egg whites until they form soft peaks. Add the sugar, a little at a time and continue to whisk until the mixture is thick and silky.

3. Gently fold in the melted chocolate, butter, ground almonds and pistachio nuts. (See page 15)

4. Place in the fridge for 1 hour.

5. Place a piece of cling film on the work surface and put the chocolate mixture on it. Use the cling film to form a 1½" diameter sausage. The cling film will make the process less messy.

6. Put a clean piece of cling film on the work surface and sprinkle the flaked almonds on it. Place the chocolate 'sausage' on it and roll it in the flaked almonds, until they are evenly distributed around the outside of the 'sausage'.

7. Roll the cling film tightly around to keep the form of the 'sausage'. Place in the fridge for 2 hours.

8. Cut into thin slices and keep in the fridge.

NOTE: Sophisticated and delicious chocolate slices. They make great after dinner treats or presents for friends.

Chocolate Log
with butter cream and raspberry jam

4 **eggs**

½ mug **sugar**

½ mug **self-raising flour**

3 tablespoons **cocoa**

Butter cream

100g softened **butter**

1 ½ mugs **icing sugar**

1 teaspoon **vanilla extract**

⅓ x 370g jar of good **raspberry jam**

1. Preheat the oven to 200°C fan oven/220°C/Gas 7. Line a 30 x 19 cm baking tray with greaseproof paper.

2. Put the eggs and sugar into a mixing bowl and whisk until the mixture is pale cream in colour and creamy in consistency. This will take about 5 minutes with an electric mixer, much longer if you do it with a manual balloon whisk.

3. Sieve the flour and the cocoa into the mixture and fold in gently.

4. Pour the mixture into the lined baking tray and cook in the oven for 12 - 15 minutes. The cake should bounce back a little when cooked.

5. While the cake is cooking, prepare to roll it when it comes out of the oven. Place a tea towel on a work surface and a piece of greaseproof paper a little larger than the baking tin and place on top of the tea towel. Sprinkle some castor sugar on the greaseproof paper. Once the cake is cooked, and while it is still hot, turn out onto the sugared paper. Using the tea towel to help you grip, roll the sponge and the greaseproof paper. The greaseproof paper should be rolled inside the sponge to stop it all sticking together. It may crack, this is not a problem. Wrap the towel round the rolled sponge until it is cool.

6. Meanwhile, mix the butter cream. Gradually add the icing sugar to the soft butter, beat well. Add the vanilla extract. The icing should be very pale.

7. Once the cake has cooled, gently unroll. Spread the butter cream evenly over the cake and then the raspberry jam. Carefully re-roll the cake and place on a plate. Dust with a little icing sugar.

NOTE: Don't just wait for Christmas to make this one, it is so scrummy. Don't worry if the swiss roll cracks as it rolls, it is just part of its rugged charm and tastes no different. Have a go!

Sweet Days

Do you steer clear of desserts because you find them intimidating to make? Have you had a string of miserable failures? Is your natural reaction to buy the dessert from the supermarket? Desserts have a 'reputation of being complicated to make', but here, I have tried to take out as much of the hassle as possible. Pavlovas always look great and really impressive. For years I thought they must be difficult to make. In this section I will show you, among other things, how to do a perfect Pavlova every time.

Strawberry Fruit Stacks
with confectioner's custard

375g pack of **ready-rolled flaky pastry**

1 **egg**, beaten

2 tablespoon **sugar**

1 punnet of **strawberries** or **raspberries**

300ml **double cream**

½ x 500ml pot **ready-made vanilla custard**

1. Defrost the flaky pastry (if necessary).

2. Preheat the oven to 220ºC fan oven/240ºC/Gas 9.

3. Take the pastry from the packet and flatten out. You should not need to roll it. Cut the pastry into 8 squares. Place the squares on lightly greased baking trays.

4. Brush the tops with the beaten egg and sprinkle the sugar evenly over just 4 squares.

5. Place them all in the oven for 12 - 15 minutes. The squares should be lightly browned and crisp.

6. Leave the pastries to cool.

7. Wash the strawberries and raspberries. Cut the strawberries into bite-size pieces if necessary.

8. Whip the cream. Once the cream is forming soft peaks, gently stir in the custard.

9. Assemble the stacks. Use a non-sugared square for the base, pile on some cream and then fruit, then put a sugared square on the top. Decorate the top with some whole pieces of fruit (see photograph).

NOTE: Foolproof and easy desserts to make for guests. Strawberries and cream always works.

| V | £0.75 /PERSON | EASE ★★★★ | SERVES 6-8 | PREP 25 MINS | FRIDGE 2 HRS |

Chocolate and Raspberry Torte
with a hint of orange

Base

½ x 300g pack of **Hob Nobs**

75g **butter** (use measures on pack)

Filling

200g **chocolate bar**

600ml carton **double cream**

rind of an **orange**

small punnet of **raspberries**

1. Crush the biscuits by putting them in a plastic bag and bashing them with a rolling pin.

2. Melt the butter in a medium saucepan. Add the biscuits and mix together.

3. Lightly grease an 8" (20 cm) round, loose-bottomed baking tin. Alternatively you can use a 20 x 13 cm oblong dish (as in photo). Line with several layers of cling film, as this will enable you to remove the tart from the dish once set.

4. Press the crumbs into the bottom of the tin or dish. Leave in the fridge while you make the filling.

5. Melt the chocolate (see page 18). Once melted, leave to one side to cool.

6. While the chocolate is cooling, whip ⅔ of the 600ml of the cream. Gently fold in the slightly cooled chocolate, being careful not to beat the mixture or you will lose the air from the cream. Add the grated orange rind and mix well.

7. Pour onto the biscuit base and spread evenly. Leave in the fridge for at least 2 hours to set.

8. Once set, whip the rest of the cream and spread over the top. Decorate with the raspberries.

NOTE: Great looking and impressive. Chocolate and raspberries with a great crunchy base.

Strawberry Pancakes
with caramel sauce

Caramel Sauce

50g **butter** (measure from the packet)

2 tablespoons brown **sugar**

4 tablespoons **cream**

1 mug **self-raising flour**

¼ mug **sugar**

4 **eggs**

½ mug **milk**

4 - 6 **strawberries**, chopped

white Flora to fry

2 large **strawberries** per person

1. To make the caramel sauce, put the sauce ingredients in a saucepan, bring to the boil and allow it to bubble gently for 30 seconds. Set to one side until needed.

2. Put the flour, sugar, eggs and milk in a bowl and mix well.

3. Add the chopped strawberries and gently stir.

4. Heat a little white Flora in a frying pan. Once hot, add the pancake mix, 2 tablespoons at a time, in order to make small pancakes. Cook one at a time, browning both sides and turning with a fish slice.

5. Serve the pancakes with the extra strawberries and the caramel sauce.

NOTE: Easy and fun to make. The caramel sauce is a little indulgent. Great if you have some kids around, however old they are!

TIP: You could also use blueberries or raspberries, instead of the strawberries.

Apple and Raspberry Cobbler
with custard

2 medium-sized **Bramley cooking apples**

2 tablespoons **sugar**

400g pack of **frozen raspberries**

Cobbler topping

2 mugs **flour**

½ x 250g block **butter**

⅓ mug **sugar**

1 **egg**, beaten and made up to ⅔ mug with **milk**

500ml carton **ready-made custard**

---

1. Preheat the oven to 200°C fan oven/220°C/Gas 7.

2. Peel and core the apples and cut into 1" chunks. Place in a pan with about ½ mug water. Gently simmer until the apples begin to soften. Add the sugar and the raspberries. Stir and pour into a casserole dish.

3. Put the flour and butter in a bowl. Rub the butter between your fingers and thumbs until the mixture resembles breadcrumbs (this will take a little bit of work).

4. Add the sugar and stir. Add enough of the egg and milk mixture to make a soft dough, mixing with a knife.

5. Turn out onto a floured board and squash into a round shape, approximately 1½" thick. Cut with round cutters or cut into 8 pieces by hand.

6. Place the pieces on top of the fruit. Brush with any leftover egg and milk mixture or just use milk. Place in the oven for 20 minutes, until the cobbler is browned.

7. Serve with custard.

NOTE: Traditional apple pie with a bit of a twist. The cobbler is easier to make than pastry and is yummy.

Mocha Moose in a Cup
with white chocolate topping

1. Mix together the coffee, water and sugar until most of the granules have dissolved.

2. Melt the chocolate (see page 18).

3. Whisk the egg whites until you can make soft peaks when you lift the whisk out.

4. In a separate bowl, beat the cream until it is thick.

5. Gently fold the chocolate into the cream, then fold in the coffee mix (see page 15).

6. Carefully fold in the egg whites.

7. Spoon into the cups and place in the fridge to set for 2 hours.

8. Sprinkle the top with grated white chocolate.

1 tablespoon good **instant coffee granules**

¼ mug **sugar**

2 tablespoons **water**

100g **dark chocolate**

2 **egg whites**

400ml **double cream**

small block of **white chocolate** (for sprinkles)

Banoffee Sundaes
with toffee sauce

1. To make the toffee sauce, put the ingredients in a saucepan and gently bring to the boil, stirring occasionally. Turn down the heat and simmer for 10 minutes until all the sugar has dissolved and the mixture thickened. Leave to cool.

2. Put the biscuits in a plastic bag and bash them with a rolling pin or equivalent 'weapon' until you have crumbs. Melt the butter in a saucepan and add the biscuits. Allow to cool slightly.

3. Whip the cream until it forms peaks (see page 15).

4. Arrange the biscuits, cream, bananas, and toffee in lots of layers in individual bowls and serve with the grated chocolate on the top. The idea behind this one is that the arrangement of the layers is fairly 'free' and rustic for a different take on the traditional banoffee pie.

½ x 300g pack **digestive biscuits**

½ x 250g block **butter**

3 **bananas**, peeled and sliced

300 ml carton of **double cream**

100g block **chocolate**, grated

Toffee sauce

⅖ x 250g block **butter**

½ mug **brown sugar**

1 mug or 1 x 397g can **condensed milk**

1 mug **double cream** (approx. 300ml)

Raspberry and Coconut Cream Mousse
with raspberry sauce

200g packet of **creamed coconut**

200g block of **white chocolate**

300 ml **double cream**

4 tablespoons **icing sugar**

2 x 225g punnets of **raspberries**

3 tablespoons **icing sugar**

1.   Take an 8" (20cm) loose-bottomed cake tin and line with cling film.

2.   Put a bowl over a pan with simmering water in it and gently warm the coconut cream and white chocolate until both melt. Leave until it is completely cooled and almost beginning to set.

3.   Whip the double cream and the 4 tablespoons of sugar until it is stiff (see page 15).

4.   Gently stir the cooled coconut cream and chocolate and one of the punnets of raspberries into the cream. The raspberries will break up a little, but try not to stir the mixture too much in order to leave some almost whole.

5.   Turn the mixture into the cake tin and press down evenly. Leave in the fridge for 2 hours.

6.   Take ¼ of the second punnet of raspberries and put them in a saucepan. Add the 3 tablespoons of sugar and 1 tablespoon of water. Heat gently for a few minutes, squashing them as you do so to get all the flavour out of them.

7.   Take off the heat, sieve and then leave the juice to cool. Add the juice to the rest of the raspberries.

8.   Take the mousse out of the fridge and turn out upside-down on to a plate. Remove the cling film. Serve with the raspberry sauce mixture.

NOTE: A light and fresh dessert. The coconut and chocolate flavours are wonderful.

WHERE ON EARTH:
Creamed coconut is not the same as coconut cream. It is in a small packet and is solid. Usually found in the 'overseas' section, near the coconut cream.

Blueberry Cheesecake
with a crunchy base

2 x 150g punnets of **blueberries**

2 x 2 tablespoons **icing sugar**

350g packet **Hob Nobs**

½ x 250g block **butter**

2 x 200g packs of **cream cheese**

300ml carton of **double cream**

juice of half a **lemon**

1. Place the blueberries in a saucepan with ½ mug water and 2 tablespoons of icing sugar. Heat gently and simmer for 2 minutes.

2. Pour into a bowl and leave until they are completely cool.

3. Put the Hob Nobs in a plastic bag and bash them around until they are very coarse crumbs, not dust.

4. Melt the butter in a pan, take off the heat and add the biscuits. Mix well. Press into the bottom of an 8" (20cm) loose-bottomed cake tin or six individual metal rings. Leave in the fridge.

5. Once the blueberries are cooled, whip the cream and the other 2 tablespoons of icing sugar until it forms soft peaks.

6. Soften the cream cheese and fold into the cream and sugar.

7. Take about ½ the blueberries out of the juice, leaving the rest in the juice. Add just the blueberries to the cream mixture along with the lemon juice. Mix gently and leave a marbled effect.

8. Spoon on top of the biscuit mixture and smooth out. Put in the fridge for 2 hours to set.

9. If you have used rings, you will need to wrap a warm cloth around each one for about 30 seconds; this melts the edges just enough to be able to slide them out. Place them on individual plates and decorate with the rest of the blueberries.

NOTE: The tartness of the blueberries and lemon create an unbelievably yummy and light cheesecake.

Baked Cheesecake
with Fruits of the Forest

300g pack of **Hob Nobs**

⅓ x 250g block **butter**

2 x 300g packets **cream cheese**

2 teaspoons **vanilla extract**

¾ mug **caster sugar**

juice of ½ **lemon**

5 **eggs**

1 mug frozen **Fruits of the Forest**

1. Preheat the oven to 180°C fan oven/200°C/Gas 6. Grease an 9" / 23 cm, loose-bottomed cake tin, line the bottom with greaseproof paper.

2. Put the Hob Nobs in a plastic bag and reduce them to large crumbs, not dust. Melt the butter in a saucepan, take off the heat, add the biscuits and mix together. Press lightly into the bottom of the cake tin. Leave in the fridge while you make the cheesecake top.

3. Put the cream cheese into a bowl and beat with a wooden spoon or electric beaters until it is soft.

4. Add the vanilla extract, sugar and lemon juice and beat until smooth.

5. Add the eggs, one at a time, beating until the mixture is smooth.

6. Pour over the biscuit mix. Place in the oven for 45 - 50 minutes until it is firm and no longer wobbles in the centre.

7. You may want to put fruit on the top. Here I have used frozen Fruits of the Forest. Put in a saucepan and add 2 tablespoons caster sugar, and simmer for 2 minutes. Allow to cool and then serve with the cheesecake.

NOTE: This is a basic cheesecake recipe. You can add any kind of in-season fruit to the top of the cake once it has cooled: raspberries, strawberries, blueberries, cherries, peaches, Fruits of the Forest and so on.

Lemon Ginger Cake
with crystalized stem ginger

300g pack **Hob Nobs**

150g **butter** (measure by the packet)

6 ready-made individual **meringues**

425ml (¾ x 600ml) carton **double cream**

2 tablespoons **caster sugar**

6 pieces of **crystallized stem ginger in syrup**, chopped finely

zest and juice of 1 large **lemon**

3 pieces of **crystallized stem ginger in syrup for decoration**

1. Place the biscuits in a plastic bag and crush with a rolling pin or similar implement. Leave the crumbs quite coarse, not dust.

2. Melt the butter in a saucepan and stir in the biscuit crumbs.

3. If you have rings, place them on a baking tray and divide the crumb mixture between them. The mixture will also fit in an 8" or 9" (20cm or 23cm) loose-bottomed cake tin. Press down the crumbs and place in the fridge.

4. Put the meringues in a bag and gently crush with your fingers, leaving the pieces reasonably large.

5. Beat together the cream and sugar until it is thick.

6. Add the ginger, meringues, lemon zest and juice and stir together. The lemon juice will cause the cream to thicken more.

7. Press over the top of the biscuit bases and level the tops. Leave in the fridge for 2 hours to set.

8. When you want to get the cakes out of the rings or the cake tin, run a cloth under the hot water tap, squeeze out and place under the baking tray, as this will loosen the bottoms. Warm the cloth again with the hot water and wrap around the sides of the rings or cake tin and the warmth will loosen the sides. Carefully remove the rings.

9. Decorate the tops with slices of crystallized ginger and a little of the syrup from the jar.

NOTE: A lovely light and zingy dessert. The odd crunch of the meringues makes it quite unusual.

TIP: You can make the ring moulds from a large plastic cola bottle. Simply cut 2" - 3" (5cm to 8cm) deep rings.

WHERE ON EARTH: Crystalized ginger and ready-made meringues are in the baking section of the supermarket.

Tangy Passion Fruit and Peach Trifles
with a zing

18 **sponge fingers**, broken in half

410g tin **peaches**

8 ripe **passion fruits**

500ml carton of **vanilla custard**

300ml carton **double cream**

juice and grated rind of a **lemon**

⅓ x 200g block **white chocolate**, chopped into small pieces

1. In each bowl, put 3 sponge fingers, 1 tablespoon of the syrup from the peaches, a few pieces of peach and the fruit from one passion fruit. (Cut the passion fruit in half and scoop out the contents).

2. Put 2 tablespoons of the vanilla custard in each bowl.

3. Whip the cream until it forms soft peaks (see page 15). Add the juice and rind of the lemon and the chocolate and stir gently. Place this over the custard in each bowl.

4. You should have 2 passion fruit left. Divide the fruit from these over the top of each trifle as a decoration.

NOTE: The strong flavour of the passion fruit is alongside the more subtle peach flavour. The occasional crunch of chocolate is a nice surprise.

TIP: Make the trifles in individual dishes if you have them. A trifle bowl is also fine.

Perfect Pavlova
with blueberries

Meringue

4 **egg** whites

1 mug **caster sugar**

Fruit: **blueberries**, **kiwi fruit**, **peaches**, **strawberries** or **raspberries**

½ pint **double cream**, whipped until it is stiff (see page 15).

1. Preheat the oven to 150°C fan oven/170°C/Gas 4.

2. Put a piece of greaseproof paper on a baking tray. A trick to stop the paper from sliding all over the place when you come to spread out your meringues is to put a few spots of oil between the paper and the tray.

3. Put the egg whites in a clean bowl, as, if there is any grease in the bowl, it will not work.

4. Whisk with the mixer until the egg whites make soft peaks.

5. Add the sugar a little at a time and keep whisking. The meringue will become 'glossy'. Don't be in a hurry; this process may take 3 - 4 minutes.

6. Once all the sugar is added, spread the meringue on the greaseproof paper (make a circle which will fit on a plate). Place in the oven for 1 hour.

7. After 1 hour turn off the oven. Leave in the oven for 20 minutes as it cools down. This makes a Pavlova which is very 'gooey' in the middle. If you like a drier Pavlova leave the meringue in the oven until the oven is completely cooled,

8. Once the meringue has completely cooled, spread the whipped cream over it and add the fruit to the top. Leave in the fridge until needed.

NOTE: People think Pavlova is very difficult to make, but as long as you use caster sugar and fresh egg whites you should succeed. You will need a food mixer to whisk the egg whites, unless you have a lot of time and are feeling very fit.

index

Thanks

This book would not have been possible without the help of many people. My husband Ron and my sons Ben and Tim have encouraged me throughout the project.

Lots of our friends have been involved in tasting the different meals in their various stages of development and giving them scores, thus weeding out the weaker recipes. Many thanks to James and Emily Malbon, Nigel and Sue Dicks, Jo Hearn, Tom Whitbread, Jess Gore, Ben & Nicole May, Jo Ingham, Amy Banham Hall, Jenni Ray, Simon William Burns, Dan Copperwheat, Ron May, Tim and Cathryn Green and Tim May.

Many thanks to all those who have been willing to be models for the photographs. They include Tom Povey, Dani Gore, Nathan Clements, Mary Jane Dorling, Payin Swazey Attafuah, Phil Hatton, Paul Davies, Dan & Jenny Copperwheat, Luke and Rachel Clements, Hannah Rycraft, Ben Whelan and Michael Whelan.

Thanks, too, to Rosy Watts for her contribution to "Rosy's Herb Garden". To see more of Rosy's work go to www.rosywatts.co.uk

Last but not least, a huge thank you to my very good friend, Fran Maciver, for her wonderful proof reading.

© 2010 Joy May

All rights reserved. No part of this book may be reproduced, stored in a retrieval system, or transmitted, in any form or by any means, electronic, mechanical, photocopying, recording or otherwise without the prior permission of the author.
Published by: Intrade (GB) Ltd
contact: joymay@mac.com
First print: May 2010
ISBN 0-9543179-5-5
ISBN 978-0-9543179-5-9
Author: Joy May
Photography and design: Tim May at www.milkbottlephotography.co.uk
Design: Ben May at www.milkbottledesigns.co.uk
Proof reading: Fran Maciver
Printed in China